TALKING TO TRUTH

An Intuition Workbook
Learn to hear, speak, and trust your UNIQUE
intuitive language

By: Anika Spencer

Talking to Truth- An Intuition Workbook

First Published in 2019

Book Cover Design by Jen Gold

Editing: Brennan Martin

yogigonerogue.com

DEDICATION

This book belongs to the hooting and hollering, come hell or high water, coo-coo cradling, hunters of jubilance that compose my support system. Thank you. Thank you. Thank you. You are the water in which I float.

CONTENTS

ACKNOWLEDGMENTS

I'd like to gratefully acknowledge all the teachers. Their shared truths form the stage on which these stories dance. Many are quoted directly, while others only in sentiment.

I'd like to thank the artists, specifically but not limited to, Ani Difranco, Buddy Wakefield, and Anis Mojgani for modeling the bravery required to be raw and reminding me that words matter.

I'd like to send appreciation to the audacious Jen Gold and the brilliant Brennan Martin. Thank you for turning this book into a work of art. Thank you, Brennan, for sharing your expertise and bringing cohesion to what was once the chaotic paint splatter of my mind in a word document.

Praise be unto Lena, Megan, Nicole, Vikki, and all the individuals who have used time and social media forums to encourage myself and others. This workbook would not exist without your expressions of faith. Your belief has made me buoyant.

I'd like to thank you, the reader, for daring to believe in your own innate wisdom and for trusting me to guide you through this process of exploration. I am honoured.

INTRODUCTION

"Your time is limited, so don't waste it living someone else's life. Don't be trapped by dogma, which is living with the results of other people's thinking. Don't let the noise of others' opinions drown out your own inner voice, and most important, have the courage to follow your heart and intuition. They somehow already know what you truly want to become. Everything else is secondary."

-Steve Jobs

While crumpled in a heap of human ache on carpet of questionable cleanliness, a certain and clear voice stated in my head, "Go to Alaska." The thought rang so crisp, I sat up straight, too shocked to cry and asked the voice, "What?" Before the word finished whizzing out my mouth, the paternal clarity interrupted. "Go to Alaska." I tried to formulate another thought and again, the same words steamrolled my mind. Shock halted the parade of pity and tempered my tears. I never again questioned the next step. I didn't know why, but I knew where. I followed the mandate of the voice in my head.

3

At the time, I was twenty-one and working full-time at a restaurant that required a white shirt and tie. I spent most days with a smile plastered on my face while fantasizing about repurposing said tie and strangling patrons who tipped ten percent on soup and salad. Recently, I'd fallen from grace. My faith in the Mormon religion hit turbulence. I'd been sent into an unavoidable tailspin (like Maverick in the classic film, Top Gun) that left me with two choices. I could go down in a ball of miserable flames on the aircraft of my religion, or I could press the eject button and brave the uncertainty of an open water landing.

I'd chosen to hit eject and found myself floundering at sea, isolated and terrified. I'd experienced the unyielding powerlessness of debilitating depression, dropped out of college, and fallen in love with my best friend who'd been inadvertently schooling me in the ways of manipulation, alcoholism, and unrequited love. All I could see was ruin. All I could do was cry. Day in and day out, I'd sob to the God I couldn't believe in anymore to save me from myself, the darkness, and the straight jacket of obsessive love. I'd pray to be freed from my addiction to a person I'll never cease to love and who never deserved my trust. On this day, He/She/It/I answered.

Maybe it wasn't "God." That's a loaded word. It swells with so many connotations that often feel limited rather than vast, dogmatic rather than curious, and rigid rather than generous. It alludes to something outside or beyond us. It reads like a rulebook written by other people, most likely men, who are now dead and, when they were alive, carried their own set of imperfections and biases. These men haven't seen inside my tender, tired, selfish heart, and if they had, they probably wouldn't have grabbed my shoulders and turned me in the direction of a train in Alaska for three summers of debauchery. The voice in my head, however, shook my shoulders and gave just such an instruction. At the time, I called that voice "God." Now, I choose to refer to this voice that speaks to me personally as Intuition.

That huge ass and awe-inspiring state of Alaska, the rustic railroad, and the collection of circus freaks that encircled my crazy with acceptance rinsed away my despondency. Those summers spun me around in dizzying and gleeful circles and, when I stopped spinning, my life danced with new possibilities. I felt found. I remained a hot mess, but a much happier one. I no longer stunk of stuck. Instead, I lived in wild rebellion and relative freedom.

Intuition and I go way back. Like any long-term relationship, our time together includes eras of tumultuousness. After the tailspin that broke my faith, I froze her out. I brandished blame and wrote the epilogue of her betrayal. Sometimes I'd deny her existence altogether. Even during these periods of feigned apathy, I knew, deep down, we were not done. Mostly this relationship could be defined as enduringly intimate. No one has stuck around longer or had my back like Intuition.

As a Mormon, I was taught to refer to this discerning inner voice as "Holy Spirit" or "The Holy Ghost." Holy Spirit's companionship was gifted to me by the hands of one of God's worthy male servants (okay, my brother) when I was eight years old. I remember expecting to feel entirely changed after this ritual initiation, but truthfully, I'd already been in communication with a wise inner voice. Eight-year-old me loved being the center of attention, and the buzzing high of my baptism revolved more around feeling cherished rather than changed. The names I use to describe my inner wisdom shift often. How carefully I listen or how quickly I apply the insight also varies, but this voice, this warm, soft, comforting blanket of protection, this bitch-slap of instinct, this adventurous trickster of a companion has spoken to me as long as I can remember. I sensed her before I received her/him as a gift at eight. I feel her now.

You might assume I'm right-brained. Some label this "highly sensitive." Many others call me crazy. (In response, I smile wickedly!) Truthfully, since birth, I've been a deeply feeling person. Consequences be damned, I'll follow my heart. I've also spent an ample amount of time in shame. I've shamed myself for the things my heart whispered before I understood them. I shamed myself for how long it took me to answer with action. I've shamed myself for my own self-betrayals and every other misstep along the way.

A friend once explained to me that in the Jewish tradition the word, "sin" in its earliest biblical translation meant "to miss the mark." We all miss the mark sometimes. We all fumble the timing. We betray the wisdom of our own soul or learn through the rigorous reaping of painful consequences. I, my friend, have withstood many a reaping.

6

Recently, my bond with my bosom buddy Intuition has deepened beyond what I previously could have fathomed. I trust her with everything I am. Our relationship is sweet and satisfying. She's the lantern I carry when exploring the creepy corners of experience. She's the MVP in my string of victories. She's with me when the guilt comes and all I can do is beg for mercy. She walks me to mountain tops and calls the wind to caress my cheeks. She's with me when I'm broken and she's with me when I'm bold. She's taken me to some weird places. Six months ago she convinced me to live out of my Buick and couch-surf for half a year. She's the gal who sent me to Alaska, and she's kept me safe through all of it.

This relationship is more important to me than any other. (Sorry, Mom, Dad, and Kat!) It's also been built the hard way. If I'm known for anything it's running towards a cliff with my heart flap open while people wildly wave their arms attempting to deter me from the leap. Leaps are my thing. So are crash landings. I wouldn't trade a single one. Your companion might not require this of you, then again, from what I hear from others, most people's Intuition seems to be both foxy and adventurous.

As a student of faceplants and crash landings, I feel compelled to share with you the truth I've extracted from all the stumbling, namely this truth: you know more than you think. You know what to do. It's okay, necessary even, to betray the voice that speaks inside of you. It's also illuminating and sublime to engage in the practice of listening for it, speaking with it, interpreting its styles of communication, and honouring this wisdom that roars and whispers. It's an exhilarating way to live. I believe that anyone with a desire can learn to hear and trust their own Intuition. It's my hope that I can aide you in your quest and help you skip any unnecessary shame in the process.

While Intuition may, at times, take the reins with a clear, crisp voice ringing audibly in your ears or loudly in your head and interrupt everything; it is more common for Intuition to speak and influence you subtly all day long. We're constantly making decisions, sometimes guided by physical information, desire, obligation, persuasion, mental constructs, or societal implications. It can be tricky. Inside of this constant barrage of decisions, we occasionally encounter small or large coincidences that feel like magic. You show up at the coffee shop late and hold the door for a beautiful stranger. A toxic relationship gets you sober. Your choice to fly home allows you to hold your grandmother a final time before her passing. A dream directs you towards a proposal. You hear song lyrics that reflect your madness. This dance twirls in us all the time.

Yet how often have you said the words, "I just don't know what I'm gonna do!" When someone asks you what your heart says have you recently responded by staring blankly? Do you know your body's favorite source of fuel? Can you distinguish between your thinking and your wisdom? Do you recognize your Intuition's voice? Can you decipher its code? Do you channel it, for yourself, or even for others? How, when, and why does your Intuition show up? When it cuts across your conscious mind and announces itself, do you trust it?

This workbook serves as a flashlight for the one who seeks to explore the cave of Intuition. It's my hope that you will not only learn to recognize your Intuition but also learn to decipher your inner wisdom's own unique and various communication styles. I hope you'll strengthen and stretch your trust muscles gaining the power to move swiftly and decisively from the place of inner knowing.

This, like all learning, will include some trial and error. It can be just as helpful to notice and learn what is not your Intuition (panic attack, anyone?), as it can be to observe the instances when Intuition presumably communicates clearly. Eventually, you'll grow your ability to contact your Intuition. You'll lob it questions, integrate its advice, and compose thank you cards and love notes in its honour.

That said, the answers and the timing of responses are rarely what we expect. You are encouraged to ask the questions anyway.

Here we go!

SECTION 1:
REMOVE YOUR HEAD

"When you reach the end of what you should know, you will be at the beginning of what you should sense."

— Kahlil Gibran, Sand and Foam

You've heard this before, but it warrants repetition: you are NOT your thoughts. Your thoughts are bountiful and probably incessant, but you are not your thinking. Hallelujah! Many of your thoughts are outright lies, diabolically cruel, numbingly redundant, or straight up outrageous. (Actually, I usually like the outrageous ones!) Most rise up so distorted by exaggeration, bias, expectation, and our natural tendency to stay on the mental prowl for circumstances that might hurt us (Danger, Will Robinson!) that while they aren't necessarily lies, they don't form a clear representation of reality, either. These thoughts, with their erratic track record,

11

deserve to be questioned. Who better to question them than you? No... not your thoughts, the raw and REAL you that shimmers and sparkles beneath and beyond your thinking.

In the spectacular decision to answer the call of my wild heart, I once drug my friend Lindsey up the notorious Mount Shasta in Northern California. It's claimed that only a third of the prospective climbers that start the trek finish the route. It's easy to see why. Aside from the daunting elevation, which exceeds fourteen thousand feet, one cannot reach the summit without traversing through snow with ice picks on a steep incline. Most hikers tackle this section while the sun is still hidden to avoid snow melt and slippery conditions. Climbers are encouraged to wear helmets as they traverse what's affectionately referred to as "the bowling alley" due to frequent rockfall. The final trudge has been aptly named "Misery Hill," and is entirely composed of loose shale that earns the climber a wiggly, dangerous backslide with every step as the rocks give way underfoot.

On the ten-hour car ride from oxygen-rich, sea-level San Diego, Lindsey and I scream-sang along to the lady-power royalty of the nineties. Alanis, No Doubt (Tragic Kingdom, of course!), and Fiona headlined. We also drew cards from my favorite Oracle Deck, an ode to Rumi by Alana Fairchild that offers the inquirer a portion of poetry and an interpretation. When Lindsey drew her card, she giggled charmingly and read to me while I drove.

"Remove your head! Not a single thread that has a head can go through the eye of needle."

-Rumi

Thirty-six hours later, wheezing, toes burning with cold, and too prideful to admit defeat, I'd become benevolently willing to turn around for a friend who'd never been this high in the sky before… (aka I was scrounging for a scapegoat). At that exact moment, Lindsey stood a hundred feet behind me bent over at the waist with her forehead resting on her icepick. I panted loudly, while looking skyward as though I could will the air above me into my body, then bellowed down at her,

"Girl! Should we turn around?"

Her pale face turned towards me and across labored breaths she responded in her singsong voice, "A while back, I put my hand on my head and I asked it what to do. It said: Screw this. Turn around. Then, I put my hand on my heart and it said: you can do this. Then, I put my hand on my gut and it said: you better fucking do this!"

To my great annoyance, Lindsey, despite all her current suffering, appeared to have removed her head. Without this response we would have surely landed in the statistical two thirds who turn around before reaching the summit of Mount Shasta. Instead, we crossed a gorgeous ice field with jagged wind carved waves of snow as high as our faces.

13

We stood (okay, laid) victoriously on the highest point of a majestic mountain alive with volcanic energy. We slid down miles of mountain on our asses through a tube-like chute of slushy August snow! That day embodied exhilaration and its memory gives rise to an immediate sense of incredible triumph.

You, too, will have to remove your head. Ironically, this undertaking will first require that you get to know your own head. Imagine you didn't know what a collar was, and someone left you a note asking you to remove it from their mastiff. You'd most likely figure it out, but initially it would involve some fumbling. Perhaps, in your uncertainty you'd avoid the task altogether. You, brave warrior, will need to meet the mind so you may remove your head. This task may sound daunting, but if this book has found you, Intuition has dubbed you ready. Fumbling and uncertainty be damned, your "decapitation" is imminent.

Onward.

If you've selected this workbook, you're probably familiar with the whole meditation thing. Unless you've been sleeping under a rock for the past twenty years you've probably heard of it. That said, are you meditating frequently, consistently, and even daily? If you are, congratulations! You're way ahead of the game! I'd even bet you and your Intuition are fairly well acquainted and ready to take it to the next level of intimacy.

Now, let's step back. I know for me, when people praise something and proclaim that I **MUST** do it, my obstinacy kicks in. I grind my heels into the ground, cross my arms, and drop like dead weight to the dirt in a childlike tantrum of refusal. Meditation is just so damn effective, I hope you surpass your possible stubbornness and test it out. It is also the launching pad for a vivid and rich intuitive practice.

Meditation doesn't have to be merely breathing. It doesn't have to be "not thinking" (although, "not thinking" is awesome!), it can be an imaginative exploration of your own psyche. It's very difficult to get to the exploration portion, however, without first honing the skill of clearing your mind of its incessant, superficial chatter. If you're new to meditation, daunted by meditation, or the proud owner of a dangerous mind that frequently launches an attack with cannonballs of anxiety or darting arrows of distraction, then I have a few "softcore" options to get you started.

At times, I've found it helpful to discard the word "meditation" and all its spiritual connotations and conjured images of Zen monks who don't represent me in all my bird-flipping, horn-honking, spaz-attacking glory. That said, the root of these practices still coincides with the guidebook of traditional methods. I'm oversimplifying and paraphrasing when I word it this way:

1. Breath. Notice your breathing.

2. Be. Notice you.

3. Notice just one thing or one part of a thing.

4. Notice everything.

5. Be everything.

(It's highly probable Patanjali is rolling over in his grave right now.)

I numbered these steps, but it might not be linear. You'll never graduate from noticing your breathing. In one sitting, you might use all five techniques or just one. That said, it's very difficult to notice or feel everything all at once when you're starting out or having a fast-paced day. There's no judgement. There's no "best." There's no "getting there." You're just here. Noticing you are here is paramount for making contact with your Intuition.

"SOFTCORE" APPROACH

ALTERNATIVE PRACTICES FOR THE RAMBUNCTIOUS AND REBELLIOUS SEEKER

Take a Bad-Ass Bath

Bath buddies can be distracting so make this a solo venture. Fill your tub with sensual pleasure. Bubbles, Epsom salt, candles, essential oils, and the water temperature of your dreams are encouraged if it amplifies your delight. Even if you don't have a candle, you may want to set the lighting low or even soak in complete darkness. (Be careful now! Tub injuries are real, yo!) Leave all electronics in a different room. You'll have enough to riff off without any music.

Once you're in the tub, feel your body. Feel the hot/warm water on your skin. Watch the tension in your muscles dissolve. Savour your scents. Close your eyes and enjoy the ease of darkness or watch the candle light flicker across your eyelids. You might want to take a few deeps breaths. (Oh, look! Step one again!) You may want to try a few different styles of breathing if they seem like they might feel good. If you're unfamiliar with breathing exercises, here's a few options you might try:

- Cleansing Breath: Draw a deep, slow breath in through your nose. Then exhale audibly out your mouth. You might try sighing as you exhale or holding the inhale at the very top. You could even sip in just a little more air before you release. For an advanced version, when finishing your exhale, see if you can empty your lungs completely. Draw the belly back and expel the last few molecules of oxygen until you can't breathe out any further. This, while uncomfortable in the moment, can turn a bland oatmeal kind of inhale into a honey, coconut, pecan kind of pleasure party. See for yourself!

- Counting: Ah! The brilliance of simplicity! You can use counting in many different ways. I know! Let's count out a few!

17

1. Watch your breathing happen. After a round of inhaling and exhaling, label the breath with a number. One. Complete another cycle of breath. That's two. Continue to count your consecutive breaths until you lose count or get distracted. This is part of it! Catching yourself in distraction is a crazy competent expression of counting breath! If or when you catch yourself distracted, start again.

2. When you're breathing in, steadily count the duration in your mind. Using the same, steady pace, count the duration of your exhale. Feel free to stop there. If you're curious about possibilities, experiment with taking more time on both sides of the breath. You might imagine the breath is trickling in and out softly like a little stream of water crawling over rocks and sand in order to find its way downhill. In the beginning, aim to keep the inhale and exhale the same length. Play with how long you can extend the breath.

   As a way to keep this sustainable, you could start with a count that feels fairly approachable. Everybody is different. This count could be five. Inhale for five counts. Exhale for five counts. Then, when you're ready, try six. Seven? Build to whatever is reachable for you today. Or don't. Much like mediation there is no THERE. It's just breath.

3. Now that you've grown proficient at breathing evenly and with counts, or to put it differently, established some equanimity, you might try on an extra layer. Add

a few extra counts to the exhale, ensuring that you are breathing out for longer than you are breathing in. For instance, you could inhale for the count of six, then exhale for the count of eight. If you're feeling coocoo for Cocoa Puffs, you could try inhaling for five and exhaling for ten. There's no right or wrong number and your internal metronome is fairly subjective. The power of this breath stems from the elongated exhale. Scientific research indicates that when our exhales exceed the length of our inhales, our parasympathetic nervous system receives the message to come online. This reminds our sympathetic nervous system or our stress response that it doesn't have to work so hard... at least, not right now. If you grew up in a home where someone held you close and told you everything was going to be okay and you believed them, then recall a time when you felt safe. A long exhale might feel similar. Just in case you didn't feel that way often or ever, or you need a reminder, allow me: (if I could hold you in my arms, I would) YOU ARE SAFE. EVERYTHING IS GOING TO BE OKAY.

- Four Part Breath: This breath has four parts. (Surprise!) One part is the inhale. The second arrives when your inhale completes itself. Before shifting into the exhale, pause. Linger in fullness. The next part is the exhale. When the exhale finishes and before the inhale begins, pause. Linger in the emptiness. This emptiness, or the space between the exhale and the inhale is the fourth part.

There are many ways to explore this breath. You don't have to count, but you might. You don't have to linger at the edges for long, but you might.

- Box Breath: Box Breath is what might happen if Counting Breath and Four-Part Breath met up for a round of pool and popcorn. (Dive bar and pool hall law requires a popcorn machine be within thirty feet of every pool table.) Bets are placed, stakes are raised, both breaths are hot and heavy and before we know it Counting Breath and Four-Part Breath are getting frisky without protection. (Please don't ask me why pool and unprotected sex go hand in hand, they just do, okay?... I'll work on it.)

  Conception aside, Box Breathing is creating a Four-Part Breath in which each part takes the same amount of time. In order to create this, you'll most likely need to count. For instance: Breath in for the count of four. Hold the fullness for the count of four. Exhale for four counts. Then, hold the emptiness for four counts. Behold, the miracle of procreation!

After a while, let go of whatever style of breathing you've decided to explore. Dramatic breathing, while useful for relaxation, can also trick you into "doing" something instead of "being" in your body in the bath. Notice your body. Notice you. Be.

Curious Coffee Drinking

Enjoy the fuck out of your morning coffee. That's basically it. I mean REALLY enjoy it. Sit down with it. Clear a space for it. Don't even take a sip from that magical mug of ambrosia until you are sitting in your coffee spot. Use the mug of your dreams! Hold a mug that's reason for creation and sole purpose is to be in your hand. I'm personally a fan of mugs that require both hands. I enjoy a mug that takes on the coffee's warmth but doesn't turn my skin pink from the heat. Make coffee drinking an intimate thing. Be a jealous lover. Set the stage so that nothing can come between you and your coffee, not your cell phone or your roommate, not even your partner, blessed be their name, if you have one. Just you. Your coffee, and your mug. It's hard to pull it off without the mug. Now close your eyes. Drink your coffee, slowly with your eyes closed. Ensure, in a way that preserves the sanctity of your pleasure fest, that this takes at least five minutes.

Disclaimer: I hear there are other beverages and substances that work for this practice. Dark chocolate, I am told, works especially well. For me, however there is only one love to be loved like this and that love is coffee. If you must use a food item, make sure it's simple enough that it can be consumed with your eyes closed. Chew slowly. Depending on the item, perhaps don't chew at all. In this exercise we are noticing one thing. Coffee, or the delight of slowly, deliberately, fully attending to pleasure.

Nature Gazing

Grab a blanket and go to the most convenient or alluring aspect of nature available to you. Consider the tree in your backyard, the sky from your local park, or the ocean, stream, or river closest to you. If it's a clear evening, star-gazing or moon-bathing could be a fabulous option. This practice is best executed outdoors but if circumstances prohibit you from leaving your home, improvise by watching rain or snow fall outside of your window, or watching flames flicker inside your fireplace.

Once you've arrived to your gazing location, get comfortable, but not so comfortable as to encourage sleeping. If you possess the gift of dropping into slumber quickly, pick a location that requires you to sit up. If you are able to remain alert and your gazing point lives upward, lie down to alleviate unnecessary strain from craning your neck. Watch the leaves rustle in the wind. Allow the radiance of the moon to land on your skin. Scan the stars. Follow the clouds as they twist and twirl. Witness the personality of the awake and ever-rearranging molecules of water. Notice this one thing. What begins as a small thing to observe, usually reveals itself as full of nuance and depth.

As you observe your aspect of nature, recognize at some point that you've stopped observing and shifted into thinking. When this happens, it is normal. It is welcome. Your recognition that thought exists is the practice. Sometimes it can be helpful to ask questions. Is this thought new, real, or helpful? Is this thought guiding you towards freedom? It is common for each of us to experience a period of mental sifting, sometimes referred to as the stage of meditation called "contemplation." Your psyche appeases your desire to clear your mind by placing at the forefront of your experience that which prohibits you from doing so. This manifests in a variety of ways: a surge of anxiety, a vivid or painful memory, or even spontaneous anger, grief, or amusement.

Leaving room for the sifting process is important. Yet the practice of "contemplation" is not a mental to-do list. It's not meal prep. It's not time spent telling yourself what a shithead you are or how terrible you are at meditation. If you've had a particular thought, dozens, hundreds, or thousands of times, and it's not paired with a new connection, it's probably not useful to you in this moment. When the option becomes available, set aside all thinking that reads boring, berating, or redundant. Lean into thinking that is liberating, new, or hopeful. Should the opportunity present itself, remove your head.

Additionally, the mind will probably attempt to organize nature. You might see a face on the moon, or images in the sky. No problema! You can use it as an opportunity to distinguish between the experiencing mind and the assessing mind. The aspect of you in charge of experiencing loves to watch clouds twist and transform and leaves blow. It enjoys observing the dance of life through the senses. The assessing mind likes to narrate and describe this experience. It's a fan of words. It's common for the assessing mind to tell you how the clouds (or other people) should have shifted. It might recommend the tree have that gnarled knob of imperfection removed. It likes to organize the world into good boxes and bad boxes.

My assessing mind likes to formulate fictitious stories about how the cloud grew angry and became nebulous out of sheer spite. It might say the cloud is out to get you. The assessing mind loves blame, hates change, and rages over minor inconveniences. The assessing mind can also be quite helpful. Its intent is usually to keep us safe. If a rattlesnake wanders right up next to you during your "softcore" meditation, by all means, channel your assessing mind to spur you to action. If no rattler is present, notice when assessment shows up in the form of judgement. Inversely, you might acknowledge when this judgement is absent.

Perhaps your mind will meander to your to-do list, the conflict in the Middle East, or Channing Tatum's six pack. Your observing, experiencing mind is the one who notices the absence of these things, their arrival, and their departure. It's the one that says, "Well, I'll be! It's Channing Tatum's six pack again!" (Apparently, your observing mind is Southern.)

Your assessing mind tends to be less genteel. It might believe your to-do list is a problem that needs to be solved immediately. It might label all conflict as "bad," or want to organize each person involved into the columns of "right" and "wrong" or "hero" and "villain." The assessing mind might love Channing Tatum's six pack, but then it wants to understand how such a wonder could exist. Maybe the assessing mind tells you that thoughts of Channing's curiously charming core are shameful or superficial. Maybe the assessor fears and fights the fleeting nature of all things, including beauty. It might proclaim that you're doing it all wrong, because you deigned to think a thought at all. The assessing mind does that, but truly, thoughts and all, you're doing just fine. The observing, experiencing mind can experience all the meandering and observe all the assessing.

When it becomes possible, gently guide your attention back to one thing, that which you came to see, nature.

Advanced practice: If contemplative practice has settled, you might jump right to number five: be everything. You, too, are a living breathing incarnation of nature. Perhaps you are just one droplet of water in the crashing wave of all that lives in this moment. Maybe, you feel connected to whatever it is you've decided to gaze upon. Maybe, just maybe, as you look at the moon you get the sense that you are the moon and the moon is you. Maybe.

Walking

Mindful walking is an oldie but a goodie. You may have been practicing mindfulness your whole life with walking. Walking meditation is actually quite traditional... sometimes done in a group by walking in a circle. You can do it in this format as well, but I prefer to walk outdoors. You are encouraged to walk slowly. Feel your feet touch the ground consciously. Acknowledge your posture. Feel free to close your eyes and navigate the world without eyesight. If you are outdoors, tread carefully. Ensure that you are in an environment that is conducive to walking with your eyes closed safely. Notice one thing: walking.

Once you've experienced full-body awareness through walking and witnessed the subtle sensations of placing one foot in front of the other, you might try on number four: notice everything. Open your eyes and notice what is around you. See your environment in small pieces, such as the crack in the pavement or the blossom on a tree or attempt to see the whole picture all at once.

It's time to move into the gritty goodness of self-examination. Throughout this book, how you tackle this process will be as unique as the terrain of self. You are encouraged to own it. Lines have been omitted to empower you to exercise your freedom. Some sections may require a scrawl, while others are better served by cursive and pretty pencils. Some of the prompts may inspire pages and pages of scratch paper full of feverish emotional purging, while others may provoke concise simplicity. I encourage you to pursue the route that facilitates the most joy and revelation. Fly free, little bird!

POST-GAME RECAP (THE WORK)

Now that you've practiced removing your head, let's review what happened. Remember, there is nothing wrong with thinking. Self-flagellation is not helpful in this context. In order to learn to recognize our thinking, we MUST think. Then, notice we are thinking, and move forward.

In order to take full advantage of the opportunity to learn from and about your mental patterns, immediately following the application of one of the above listed "softcore" practices or directly after a traditional seated meditation, log your experience by answering the questions below (grab extra paper if you need).

How do you feel?

Were you able to "remove your head"? Did you notice moments or windows of time in which thinking was absent? Please convey the details.

Recall any specific thoughts you became aware of during your practice. How often did this specific topic draw your attention?

At any point, did you find yourself in "contemplation" or "sifting" through that which prohibits you from removing your head or accessing a peaceful moment? If so, what were you sifting through or contemplating? How did you distinguish this to be the beneficial process of cleaning the mirror of the mind as opposed to regular old routine thinking?

Did you experience bliss or clarity? Tell me about it!

If you're new to this, the first few attempts tend to reveal the brain to be a little wily. Don't worry! It takes a little practice, but the payoff is fabulous. (I mean, if you're into payoffs like peace, contentment, and freedom.) Let's try again!

How do you feel?

Were you able to "remove your head"? Did you notice moments or windows of time in which thinking was absent? Please convey the details.

Recall any specific thoughts you became aware of during your practice. How often did this specific topic draw your attention?

At any point, did you find yourself in "contemplation" or "sifting" through that which prohibits you from removing your head or accessing a peaceful moment? If so, what were you sifting through or contemplating? How did you distinguish this to be the beneficial process of cleaning the mirror of the mind opposed to regular old routine thinking?

Did experience bliss or clarity? Tell me about it!

Once more for the cheap seats in the back!

How do you feel?

Were you able to "remove your head"? Did you notice moments or windows of time in which thinking was absent? Please convey the details.

Recall any specific thoughts you became aware of during your practice. How often did this particular topic draw your attention?

At any point, did you find yourself in "contemplation" or "sifting" through that which prohibits you from removing your head or accessing a peaceful moment? If so, what were you sifting through or contemplating? How did you distinguish this to be the beneficial process of cleaning the mirror of the mind as opposed to regular old routine thinking?

Did experience bliss or clarity? Tell me all about it! (I'm a geek for bolts of bliss and flashes of clarity!)

SECTION 2:
THE REALM OF FEELINGS

"I believe in intuitions and inspirations... I sometimes FEEL that I am right. I do not KNOW that I am."

— Albert Einstein

If you are like me, at times, you might feel like a big ball of feelings. Then again, maybe you don't. The experience of emotion for each individual can display across a vast spectrum. A friend of mine relayed to me her experience of couples counseling. In their sessions, she and her partner were working to enhance their understanding of one another through communication. She'd assumed before their sessions that her partner was refusing to share his emotional experience with her due to a fear of vulnerability. What emerged, however, was not a lack of desire to expose his emotional

35

realm, but rather a difficulty in recognizing sensations as emotions as well as a lack of language to describe and communicate these experiences.

As a deeply feeling person, this account shot bits of my brain out my ear holes! We **DO NOT** all feel, register, and interpret emotion the same way. Feelings are not gendered, but our culture often trains each gender to synthesize emotion differently. In this example and commonly, women are more encouraged to sense and speak of the experience of emotion. No matter where you fall of the "feeling spectrum," we, all at some point in our lives, (for myself, it might be daily!) repress our emotions, misinterpret our feelings, or overly identify with and cling to certain explanations.

All feelings are valid. They are allowed to be here. Some emotions are a part of your intuitive alert system. Others are responding to your current line of thinking. Some are run-of-the-mill emotions that we each experience daily. In order to build a stronger relationship with your own brand of Intuition, you'll want to learn to distinguish between feelings that are a natural, normal part of living, feelings that are responding to mental constructs, and feelings that reveal feedback from your unconscious and subconscious. Here are some questions that might help you along...

THE GROUNDWORK

Please name your current emotion. There may be a variety of layers or textures. For instance, intense joy can be scary. Despair can feel muted. Anger often masks sadness. Like a spelunker with a headlamp, curiously navigate the entire experience. Explore the whole cave. Go into its depths. No matter what you find, steer clear of labels like "good" or "bad." Whatever the emotion, it's a guest... not a permanent tenant. Don't leave any aspect of your experience out in the cold.

Where are you experiencing the sensations of emotion in your body? Describe your physical experience. Are you at ease? What areas, if any, hold tension, sensation, or discomfort? Is any area of your body off-line, numb, or unperceivable? Are you comfortable? How alert do you feel? How, if at all, do you interpret this in terms of emotion?

Is your current emotion visceral? Are there butterflies in your belly? Are you nauseated? Does your abdomen feel tight, bloated, cramped or loose? Describe your digestion. What does your gut say?

How are you breathing? Is it shallow and uncomfortable? Are you short of breath? If you consciously breathe more slowly, does it change? Does your chest feel restricted or open and broad? Are you wary of turning your chest and face directly towards someone? Does it hurt? Do you wish to sigh, sing, or sway?

What about your heart? Is it pounding? Can you hear it? Feel it? Can you perceive the back of your ribcage? Is there a strong desire to press your back up against a wall or other protective surface? Are your shoulders rounded forward? Do you feel confident?

Are there sensations in your throat? Are you currently touching it? Do you panic when this place is touched? Do you perceive mild or prominent constriction? Does this moment remind you of choking? Are you grinding your teeth? Do words flow freely and easily? Do the sounds around you grate on your nerves? Can you easily listen and retain what's being said? Is there insight being gathered from what is not said? Are you speaking to discharge discomfort? Does your body fear your words do not have value? Do your words ring true? How can you tell?

List any additional insight you've extracted as you've explored and described the experience of this emotion:

There are times when our body communicates wisdom. There are also times when our body responds to our current line of thinking. Approximately a year after a soul-shattering and life-changing break up with an alcoholic, I was sitting in a warehouse in Southern California, by myself, performing menial tasks for a friend who'd started her own food packaging company. While alone in this room with white walls and buzzing lights, my mind wandered to my most recent love. I was suddenly seized by the physical experience of fear as the thought rung in my mind, "What if he's dead?" If you've ever deeply loved an alcoholic or an addict, then you understand the trial of this looming question. Suddenly, the thought changed from a question into an assertion. "He's about to die. I can feel it. Something is terribly wrong."

A spasm of tears flooded my eyeballs, and I pitched my head forward and between my knees so that the salty liquid could drop directly from my eye sockets onto the cement floor. We, women, do strange things to avoid smudging our eyeliner. I recognized in the moment that this irrational outburst could probably be identified as a panic attack. For no reason based in reality, my mind convinced my body that someone I once loved was about to die. My body responded accordingly, spraying me (and the room) with urgent grief. I struggled to breathe for the next forty-five minutes and in the aftermath, I ached for answers. I desperately wanted to know why.

Why do some of us live long, healthy, relatively charmed lives while others burn at both ends until they're nothing but ashes? Why must some children face atrocities? It is easy to see why my own suffering is necessary and useful but when I look at the imprints of terror and cruelty in the lives of others, that theory seems quite feeble. What, in a world full of fear and pain, is the point? What is the meaning of all this living? These are time old questions. They crashed into me like a fifteen-foot wave swallowing an amateur surfer. They pulled me into the depths, stole my breath, and somersaulted me until I didn't know which way was up.

My point is... we all have runaway brains. Sometimes those brains take us down dark rabbit holes that lead us into vortexes filled with remorse, worry, and the imminent arrival of the worst possible circumstances. This rabbit hole is not Intuition. It is the quicksand of debilitating fear. Fear that we are beyond redemption, fear that it's up to us to stop the tide of the world and we are failing, fear that tragedy will strike or that we won't be able to weather it when it does.

Your Intuition doesn't deal in this kind of communication. If danger is present, legitimate, or tangible, your Intuition won't strike with grief (at least not right then) or worry. She'll strike with clarity. She responds to danger with calls to action, swift changes in direction, and, at times, searing anger and instinctual reactions. If it seems like life and death, and you aren't called to action, it's probably fear. If you suddenly and inexplicably have a razor-sharp focus, Intuition is calling.

"Do not worry, but know that worry is as effective as trying to solve algebra equations by chewing bubble gum. The real problems in life are apt to be things that never crossed your worried little mind. The kind that blindside you at four pm on some idle Tuesday."

-Baz Luhrman

Let me be clear. Worry is not your Intuition. Let me state this again, because it's worth repeating. **WORRY IS NOT YOUR INTUITION.** Your Intuition doesn't have time for worry because it's too busy delivering the messages that are pertinent to you right now in real time. Intuition might deliver messages that are so wildly out there that you begin to worry about how, in the name of everything living underneath the light, that could possibly take place. Furthermore, how the hell are you going to get through it if does? It might tell you things you don't want to hear or know, but Intuition, in and of itself, does not show up in the form of worry... nor does it require that you stress out over the information it delivers.

For example, Intuition might give you a gentle nudge to call your Dad and tell him that you're sorry, that you love him, and to thank him for all the things he did to create the person you are today. Whether Pops passes away tomorrow or at the ripe age one hundred and twelve, you'll probably be glad you shared that conversation. If, however, the thought strikes you that your father is dead or dying and there's nothing you can do about it, well that's probably not your Intuition. It's not helpful. It's not hopeful. It isn't motivating, inspirational, or bringing you peace.

It's just fear. If anything, Intuition wants you to clear your mind and embrace what's coming. In order to ease you into that transition, it's likely to coax you in with feelings of warmth, love, calm, or enthusiasm. The package from Intuition might not match what you thought you ordered on Amazon. Maybe it's exactly the item you picked out, but once it's assembled you realize you'd rather sell off your furniture and move to Zimbabwe. Either way, Intuition is rooting for you. It's sure that you are meant to bodybuild your inner badass and thus guides you and your tired, worried, little mind into exactly the scuffles you need to live out your own legend.

I think many of us have followed a "never to be validated as wise" impulse to take a different path. Perhaps you've mentally time-travelled to the past and caught a glimpse of the fate that waited had you chosen differently or if your choices hadn't been stripped from you. For me, that fate looks like being a young mother with a picket fence and life of Mormonism. It also looks like depression and divorce, but who's to say? Most of us will never know what was down the trail we never took.

Let's assume each of us has done the best we can to hear and heed our Intuition up to this point. For the sake of sanity, give yourself the benefit of the doubt and presume that you've been guided, consciously or unconsciously to right here, right now. Assume because you are here, and because assuming anything else is basically torture, that Intuition has brought you to this exact trail. You can't teleport to a different place on the map, but you and your Intuition can work as team to determine which direction or path you'll head down next and when you'll depart.

It's my own opinion that anger can be a preserving incarnation of Intuition, although I think it depends on the brand of anger and our own dispositional tendencies. For instance, I've spent a decent chunk of time working in restaurants. It's common, normal even, for co-workers to place their hands on each other's backs when passing behind one another. To be honest, there's also been a good amount of ass-slapping over the years, which was okay for me, until it wasn't. Somewhere along the line, I started placing a higher premium on my personal space. That said, the perfunctory touch of someone's hand is commonly a part of the business.

Regardless, when the employee who spent more time with his eyes on my body then my face placed his hand on my back, then stumbled over the rubber floor mats and grasped for my arm without relinquishing, I didn't have time to grapple with whether my response was kind or even appropriate. Instead I jerked my hand away and turned my rage on the person who stood easily despite the pull of my momentum. My lips curled into a snarl, "Don't you fucking touch me." I growled.

Intuition? Maybe. Some people might believe there's no such thing as righteous anger. Much like the untaken pathway, I'll never know what the effects of a more demure response might have been. I choose to believe that all our emotions have their place. Anger, although often misplaced, also tends to play a role in keeping us safe.

Some feelings don't have to pound as furiously to be heard. Joshua Tree National Park has long reigned as the local king of crags for climbing, camping, and communion. On an excursion to the luminous desert, I took the three-hour drive alone with the intent to meet up with a friend and his current girlfriend. The car ride to this mecca was miraculous. I didn't even need music or an audiobook, I just sat alone with myself in sweet serenity for three luscious hours. When I arrived into the park, this serenity popped like a bubble. I scanned the scraps of paper pinned to the message board of the most coveted campground for my name. Instead, I found a message to my friends from their other comrades that read:

"Chris and Britt!! Meet us at Jumbo Rocks Site twenty-one and twenty-two for brews and boulders!" When I located the campsite, it was abandoned. I let my dreams of traversing climbs crumble and walked out into the gravelly desert. I dropped my pack, took off my shoes, and immediately meandered mentally back into serenity. Yet again, no music, no distractions, just the sunlight on my body and the soft wind brushing the earth. I leaned and lounged on the small pebbles and let the desert warmth sweep over my bare legs and arms.

As a smiled at the satisfaction of solitude, I wrote a letter to myself from the desert. I realized, I didn't want to find my friend and his innumerable comrades. Despite the fact that I was relatively new to sobriety, I didn't think I'd be tempted to consume alcohol simply because they partook. Still, it also didn't sound like much fun to attempt to connect with strangers who gave brews billing over boulders. It's not that I didn't like brews, I loved them. That's how I'd gotten into this whole sobriety pickle in the first place!

I looked up at the sun. I felt into my body. Truth be told, I didn't want to socialize. I didn't want to be the sober one in what was once my favorite brand of a party. I wanted to be alone. I laced my shoes, picked up my pack, and snuck past the abandoned campsite. My decision was reaffirmed when I cringed at the thought of the group returning before I made my getaway. I drove the three hours back home. My decision felt solid. A month later, I got my "intuitive confirmation." A different friend relayed that the couple I'd intended to meet broke off their relationship in an uproarious drunken argument. Their coupling exploded the same evening I'd side-stepped our meet-up. One member of the party spent most of the night in a belligerent black-out. Praise be unto my Intuition! Hallowed be Her name!

My point is two-fold. Firstly, many intuitive impulses never play out to our full comprehension. Other times, we immediately or eventually find evidence that our crafty Intuition clearly corralled us towards safety, wellness, or growth. The times when we heed Intuition and get confirmation provide excellent opportunities for observation. We also learn from totally ignoring these insights and observing the consequences. If we act and never have our intuitive premonitions and choices confirmed with the clarity of evidence, it can still strengthen our steadiness. I call those types of insights: learning to trust yourself without the requirement of outside validation.

Secondly, emotions and feelings can be a powerful part of intuitive language. A sharp sense of danger, searing hot rage, and a craving for privacy are just a few examples. Some of my own personal favorites also include: the sensation of my soul singing when I visit certain places, deep connection and intimacy with a freshly found or revisited friend, statements that ring so beautiful or so true you gasp, feeling like you've known someone since the dinosaurs roamed, and the satisfaction and exhaustion of a day well spent.

To reiterate, some feelings are just feelings. Some feelings are provoked by our thinking. Some feelings are straight gold. You can take them to the bank.

Let's examine some of your past emotional experiences to see if we can find a trend that helps you better speak the emotional language of Intuition. When we take the approach of learning from our past experiences, it can be helpful to eliminate the need to label these experiences as "good" or "bad." Continue to find value in learning what your intuitive language is NOT as you hone your understanding of what your Intuition actually, truly is. Let's start with anger.

As you examine how anger has affected your well-being, you might feel compelled to describe how you believe your anger has affected other people. When we are the cause unnecessary harm to someone we love or value, our own well-being often suffers. It can be confusing, however, to focus too much on the other person, since we may brush up against the shame and unrealistic expectations often associated with anger. This isn't to imply that the harm we cause to others isn't worthy of our attention, yet for the sake of simplicity and in order to remain focused on the purpose of this exercise, you are encouraged to focus on how your anger has affected you personally rather than postulating on how someone else may or may not have interpreted or internalized the event.

THE WORK

Describe a time when anger or the way you expressed your anger sabotaged your well-being:

Log an instance in which anger preserved your safety or well-being, helped you shed harmful behaviors or relationships, cauterized the wound in your emotional healing process, or another beneficial incarnation of anger.

What were the noteworthy differences between these two examples? How was the quality of the anger different? State any prominent thoughts, fears, or deeply rooted beliefs that contributed to your anger.

In the name of clarity, let's investigate a new set of scuffles with anger.

Describe a time when anger or the way you expressed your anger sabotaged your well-being:

Log another instance in which anger preserved your safety or well-being:

What were the noteworthy differences between these two examples? How was the quality of the anger different? State any prominent thoughts, fears, or deeply rooted beliefs that contributed to your anger.

Take three!

Describe a time when anger or the way you expressed your anger sabotaged your well-being:

Log an instance in which anger preserved your safety or well-being.

What were the noteworthy differences between these two examples? How was the quality of the anger different? State any prominent thoughts, fears, or deeply rooted beliefs that contributed to your anger.

Now, let's try sadness. I know! This probably isn't the transition you were looking for seeing as anger is frequently a sadness shield. When examining the darker side of our experience, I sometimes find it helpful to visualize myself as a warrior or an explorer. You are not weakened by your sadness, you are strengthened by it. Every exploration has tribulations. Hell, I can't even take a road trip without getting lost. I recently made plans to meet friends in Baja and left San Diego solo at six o'clock pm on a Friday night. Ten minutes after I crossed the border, I realized I was lost in Tijuana on a one-way street, alone, at night. I spoke very little Spanish and understood even less. It took me an hour and two near death experiences on roundabouts, before I finally waved the white flag of surrender and heading towards what I thought was home. By the magical powers of surrender, I instead found myself on the roadway I'd sought in the first place. That's the thing about exploration. It's tricky. It's uncomfortable. It's scary. We return more aware of our shortcomings and more resilient having faced them.

My brief collegiate career took place at Brigham Young University in Provo, Utah. In my third semester of college, I had... well, it might be best described as a devastating break-down. Depression haunted my adolescence. I suspected it was some burrowing parasite I'd contracted that grew larger and more powerful each time it was named. I'd fantasized about suicide. It would be so sweet to slip away. It was solely the fear of hell, not my love for life, that kept me rooted to this planet. No one suspected. I wasn't that kind of sufferer. People often described me as a beacon of light, but some nights I could barely breathe inside the darkness. No one suspected that was, until the breakdown.

College is hard. Maybe, it's my attention span, but I think the reality is, it's just hard. I felt lost and unknown. In response to this sense of isolation, I crawled deeper into the dark cave of my dorm room, on the fourth floor where the boys were banned. (They weren't allowed on any floors, aside from between the hours of five pm and seven pm on Wednesdays.) I watched hours and hours of Smallville. I wanted to be loved the way Clarke loved Lana. I desperately desired to BE desperately desired instead of someone no one wanted.

I wanted a life that looked like a TV show, not a dingy dorm room with stained gray carpet that protruded and tripped me in certain places and a dresser too small to hold my secrets and my doubts. I despised class. I was bored there, and I had no real motivation behind my studies. I'd enrolled in college because it was the prescribed next step. In my mind and according to my upbringing, you went to college, so you could get an education, so you could get a great paying job. Well, that's not entirely true. Not only did I attend a Mormon college, I'd been a practicing Mormon my entire existence.

It is the cultural norm among families that are members of the Church of Jesus Christ of Latter-Day Saints (commonly referred to as Mormons) to raise children, sometimes whole flocks of children. It is encouraged that the women of the faith make child-rearing their full-time job. It's considered the honour and obligation of the woman to see to the to task of loving and attentive child care. It is explicitly stated by this faith that a woman's place is in the home. A woman's education was a placeholder or a back-up plan, should she fail to wed. I attended a university geared toward giving me an education, but also, a husband. I was eighteen and my lack of dating greatly concerned a good many people, myself included.

Despite the cultural pressures to pursue motherhood first and personal development second, I'd always been both devoted to the faith and a little deviant. I desperately sought to live according to the precepts the religion laid out for me, but I also frequently fell just a little bit short, sometimes hella short. My rebellious side kept derailing my ambition to be righteous. It was a source of both pride and shame that I'd already dabbled in smoking, drinking, swearing, and "heavy petting" (the term used in the official church statement that quantified making out with a little extra, as a sin).

As a result, I'd been left perpetually restless, dissatisfied, and ashamed of myself. I didn't feel like I belonged. I couldn't imagine belonging anywhere else. I didn't know how I wanted to spend my life, but I knew I didn't want to be a mother by the end of next year, like most of the freshmen girls on my floor, some of whom were currently engaged.

So, I did what I'd been taught to do. I kept moving. Until I couldn't. Until I didn't. Until, I was lying in bed, a crying heap and I couldn't get up, for a week. On day three, my friend Kelli, who I'd known since I was three tried to crack the door open in order to coax me to come out. I threw a shoe at it. My roommate tried to get me to leave the room. I told her to "fuck off!" (how un-Mormon of me!) After seven days of doing nothing but sleep and cry, I got up. I didn't go far.

I realized it was hard to sleep in a dorm room with a window as tall as the ceiling in the middle of the day. So, I moved to the common room. The common room was only used at night. It had no windows. I could sleep there all day. And I did, or at least, I slept there often. I did start moving around some, but the act of walking to a class seemed unfathomable. Class was excruciating. It was a fate worse than death: boredom. I believe I turned up for my biology final, but I didn't do well, shockingly. Life seeped back in through socializing. I started to move again, to go to parties and make out with boys. I loved me some heavy petting. It was with one of these boys, that I broke down crying and finally said the words:

"I don't know if I can do this anymore. I don't know if I believe in the church. I don't think I can live this way AND be happy." I'd told him because I'd thought that he was a rebel like me. I thought he was a doubting, rule-breaker, who wanted to be good but couldn't. Instead, he tried to teach me. He told me he knew the church was true. He offered and gave me a priesthood blessing. In the Mormon religion men are given the power of God, and thus can deliver God's blessing through this power by placing their hands on a person's head and praying. The idea that I needed a man's hands in order for God to bless me was part of my intellectual problem with the religion in the first place, but I accepted the blessing anyway.

Neither his masculinity nor his blessing saved me from becoming forsaken. Instead, the doubts grew stronger and stronger and stronger. My actions and focus took me further and further and further from the religion. My "friends" from church started to keep their distance from me as though I'd contracted something contagious. The further I moved away, the more functional I became. I quit school. I moved off campus. I started working. I dated.... poorly. Finally, it happened. Something broke. I couldn't stomach it anymore. The darkness came and it took me, again. This time I sat in the parking lot of Gold's Gym, body racked with waves of sadness as any residual faith in this Mormon God poured out my eye sockets.

I pulled out my Nokia and dialed the busser at my restaurant. He spoke so intelligently about God. I'd spent hours rolling silverware and listening raptly as he expounded on the topics of philosophy and religion. Surely, if anyone could explain this to me, he could. I begged him. I begged him to explain. I begged him to tell me how God could see men and women so differently. How gender could matter to someone like God. In my mind, if the founder of Mormonism or the following prophets could get one thing wrong, if they missed just once, then that nullified everything. I begged him, but even the smartest person I knew, the most philosophical and the least judgmental couldn't explain it to me. A true academic, he didn't pretend he could.

That was the night I lost my religion.

It's fine.

Honestly, it's better than fine now. It's great! I am so grateful for this gut-wrenching bout of depression. It's not that every person's depression is communicating with them (or maybe it is, I don't know). I just know mine was communicating with me. Some moments are sad. Sometimes, we just feel blue. It's okay. Other times (and this is also okay) our sadness is communicating with us as the voice of Intuition. It could be saying something like: "Hey you! Get off your duff and get out into the world and interact with some other humans!" It might be letting you know that your current job is sucking the soul right out of you. Your subconscious could be sending you hints that you currently have a toxic way of thinking or that your actions are WAY out of line with your values.

I do not believe that we are meant to be miserable. Due to this belief, sustained sadness (not to be confused with grief) could be an indication that your soul yearns for you to shift how you see the world or how you show up in it. For me, I needed to leave a religion and reformulate my beliefs. Good grief, some days I feel like that process will never be over! (Maybe, death?) Perhaps, you just need to get more sleep, or seek the help of a professional who can help you identify and reshape some problematic thinking. Maybe you require a vacation, more play, alone time, or a fantastic sexual encounter!

Just like anger, not all sadness requires action. Your task in deciphering the intuitive language sometimes spoken by your feelings is to grow better at recognizing which feelings are meaningful and communicative and which are not. Much like anger, steer clear of shaming your sadness, or speaking to how we presume others might feel due to your expressions or actions around said sadness. Instead, focus on how you believe this affects you, since you are the very best equipped person to distinguish the nuances of your own experience.

THE WORK

Recount a time when sadness or the way you handled or held onto your sadness sabotaged your well-being:

Log an instance in which sadness aided you in your quest for well-being, helped you shed harmful behaviors or relationships, communicated valuable lessons, or revealed a strength or super power:

Chronicle the noteworthy differences between these two examples. How was the quality of the sadness different? What were the thoughts, fears, or deeply held beliefs surrounding them. How long were these experiences of sadness and what factors contributed to the length of time?

Again, please!

Recount a time when sadness or the way you handled or held onto your sadness sabotaged your well-being:

Log an instance in which sadness aided you in your quest for well-being:

Chronicle the noteworthy differences between these two examples:

Charmed, I'm sure you are. (Thank you, Yoda!)

Recount a time when sadness or the way you handled or held onto your sadness sabotaged your well-being:

Log an instance in which sadness aided you in your quest for well-being:

Chronicle the noteworthy differences between these two examples:

The good news is Intuition can also speak through joy. Just like the darker side of feelings, not every flash of fun is an intuitive marker. Not every person who enjoys the sound of music or strumming a guitar is being called to become a musician. Then again, some are.

Passion, excitement, and exhilaration often arrive to beckon us in the direction of our next great adventure. Frequently, it's not the adventure we expect. Intuition can be similar to that "life of the party" friend, the one who asks you along for a joyride to the post office and the next thing you know you're getting your picture taken on a donkey painted like a zebra in Tijuana. (Yeah. It's a thing.)

Here's a more practical example. In my late twenties, my excitement mounted around the idea of returning to school. I spent the next year and a half dabbling in various classes at community college. I learned a decent amount. I also learned a lot about what makes a superb, or less effective, teacher. I became re-acquainted with the format of college education. Not long after my academic meandering, I applied for a job teaching yoga at San Diego State University. It was suggested that I apply to teach some of the curriculum classes offered by the university. My recent experience at community college not only helped me feel confident in the interview, but in some ways prepared me for the task of teaching at the college level. In no way did this match the expectations I had when I registered for "Theories of Consciousness" three years earlier. Yet my

Intuition had my back and these small bursts of passion lit my path through unexpected terrain.

Sometimes I refer to these little flashes of excitement, motivation, or opportunity as "The Golden Threads." Imagine glancing down at the dirt and a flash of brightness catches your eye. You reach down to investigate and discover it's a gleaming golden thread, buried in the earth. You pull on it and it emerges from the ground. The string extends out of sight and into the distance, leading down a random path you hadn't previously considered. You don't know where it leads but you follow it because it's there and you're curious and it's beautiful. You might even follow this thread until it ends. In contrast, your enthrallment with an idea or a person might fade as you recognize reality and your own motivations. You might love the original path so passionately and steadily, you don't have time for strings. Perhaps it's the prestige or the reward that draws you to a project, not the endeavor itself. Perhaps you realize a romantic allure stemmed from feeling chosen or validated rather than from attraction and appreciation for another person in their wholeness. At least, these are some of my confusions. Your list may be different.

Expectations can make golden threads appear as dingy, yellow, dirty strings better left untouched. If you follow one exciting possibility to its end and wind up in a field of wheat in the middle of Kansas, when you'd thought you were headed to a luxury resort in the Bahamas, you probably won't find the field very satisfying or even interesting.

On the other hand, if you happened upon this field at golden hour, only to watch your companion rush behind the curtain of grain and beckon you to follow, you might have a totally different relationship with the field. I don't mean to downplay the value of ambition. However, it's my experience that it's easier to have fun along the way when I'm not obsessing over the destination.

As you explore the emotions of passion and excitement as expressions of Intuition. Please note the expectations you had of the situation and how that played into the outcome and your assessment.

THE WORK

Recall a time when excitement, desire, passion, or the way you handled these emotions sabotaged your well-being:

Log an instance in which excitement, desire, or passion aided you in your quest for well-being. Was it joyful unto itself? Did it blow motivation into your sails? What lights you up?

Describe the noteworthy differences between these two examples. How was the quality of the excitement different? Did you follow the golden thread? Did greed, lust, or craving contribute? How did expectation play into your ability to enjoy what unfolded?

Again, with gusto!

Recall a time when excitement, desire, passion, or the way you handled these emotions sabotaged your well-being:

Log an instance in which excitement, desire, or passion aided you in your quest for well-being.

Describe the noteworthy differences between these two examples. How was the quality of the excitement different? Did you follow the golden thread? Did greed, lust, or craving contribute? How did expectation play into your ability to enjoy what unfolded?

TALKING TO TRUTH

Recall a time when excitement, desire, passion, or the way you handled these emotions sabotaged your well-being:

Log an instance in which excitement, desire, or passion aided you in your quest for well-being.

Describe the noteworthy differences between these two examples. How was the quality of the excitement different? Did you follow the golden thread? Did greed, lust, or craving contribute? How did expectation play into your ability to enjoy what unfolded?

Now, let's circle back. Visit your own personal Joshua Tree. Perhaps you take a literal pilgrimage to the place that kick-starts your heart and your inner poet. You may decide to stay right where you are, close your eyes, and visually travel to this location. Then pretend **YOU ARE the place**, the desert, the house you grew up in, the mountain, the ocean, the seething city that lights you up. Then write a letter to yourself from this place. Tap into your childhood skill of pretending, my friend! Practice making shit up and see what happens.

SECTION 3: MAKE IT HURT!

"At times you have to leave the city of your comfort and go into the wilderness of your intuition. What you'll discover will be wonderful. What you'll discover is yourself."

— *Alan Alda*

In the grand crescendo of the wildest romantic ride I'd ever been on, I found my ex-heroin addict of a boyfriend under a bridge (like a troll). This bridge was part of a walking path that stretched a part of ocean that cradles San Diego and drew a young homeless community since it was isolated from the roadway and therefore rarely patrolled. I'd gone to the desert with a few girlfriends for the weekend, (Joshua tree, of course!) yet I'd spent most of it pining for my love. I'd driven out to find cell phone service the day before and expressed my excitement at being reunited the next day. I said the words, "I'll see you tomorrow morning! I love you so much!"

79

When I returned, he was nowhere. The house bore all the signs of a bender; bottles everywhere, clothing strewn about, a pair of worn lady's underwear included. I texted to inquire about their location. Nothing. I called his phone. No answer. I waited. I felt awash with fear. I seethed. Since I could not sit still and thinking was dangerous, I stood up and took my ass to yoga.

When I'd finished class, I found a voicemail. In a voice that seemed miles away he asked if I could find him and his troupe mushrooms. That was it. No location. No information. Just a question. Yet when I dialed him back, no answer. I explained to his voicemail that I was upset. I sent a text outlining my frustration. He responded by texting a location, which was where I found him, eyes bloodshot, no shoes, under a bridge, on the beach, chilling with an old army buddy, another woman whose underwear I'd recently encountered, and a homeless youth.

Up until this point, all our greetings involved me running to land in his arms because I couldn't wait a second longer to be touching. I'd been working nights at a restaurant three blocks from our house and on my walk home he'd meet me halfway. His mouth would widen in a boyish grin and he'd open his arms wide to receive the momentum of my excitement. He'd kiss me, passionately, without apology, without reserve. He did not change who he was or temper what he wanted because someone else might be watching and feel uncomfortable. When it came to me, I loved this. When it came to alcohol, I resented it.

It was a testament to how far away we were from one another when he didn't rush to me upon my arrival to the beach. In fact, he didn't even get up. In truth, he barely looked at me. As though focusing his eyes or lifting his lids enough to see beyond the sand on the side of his right foot exceeded his strength. He could only feign to try.

My love, my person, who'd long been locked inside a box full of tattered, musty blankets, who frequently found himself gagged and muffled by addiction no longer thrashed to free himself. He didn't even move. He couldn't lift his body or his eyes to meet mine. He sat there staring at the sand by the side of his right foot. He quickly grew frustrated and disdainful of my questions and the anger granted him the strength to whip his head to one side and lift his faded, red rimmed, blue eyes towards me.

"Jesus. I already said I was sorry. What do you want from me?" What did I want? I wanted to talk to my lover, not his belligerent counterpart. I wanted to annihilate this white, hot rage. I wanted the girl whose panties currently rested on my apartment floor to not be present while my boyfriend responded to my feelings with impermissible dismissiveness.

I walked down to the ocean to stare at the waves in hopes that the sight of the water would douse the fire that burned in my gut. I hoped my ears would stop ringing and the tyranny of frustration pounding in my skull would subside. I also wished he would muster the ability to lift his weary body, walk out from underneath the bridge, and face me like two humans living in real time, instead of floating in alternate realities of rage and absence.

Despite my deep breaths and the balm of the ocean, my fury and fear did not abate. My love did not lift the burden of his body to come to me. Instead, I heard him laugh, a sound that nearly exploded my brain given the context. I trudged through the sand to square off to him. I approached and through struggling breath asked is we could talk privately. Then, a dripping wet, tattooed youth emerged from the ocean. He ambled up to our tense and distant group and directed his attention to the homeless youth who sat between my love and the girl with missing panties. He pulled a needle from his back pocket and proclaimed,

"Ah hell! I jumped in with my stash."

This is approximately the moment when I lost my shit.

My ex-heroin addict, retired bar brawler, unemployed, booze-addled, marijuana dependent boyfriend managed to drag himself into the standing position and slowly followed my quick steps away from our group onto the cement path that curved around the shoreline. (He hated it when I walked faster than him.) When we were beyond hearing distance, or at least we would have been if we weren't about to be shouting, I turned on my heel and waited for him to approach. I set my jaw, looked into the tired and angry face of my six foot seven inches of a man and screeched,

"What the fuck are you doing!?!? You're down here sleeping on the beach with people who have heroin needles in their back pockets! You knew I was coming, and I haven't been able to get a hold of you for hours! I left at five am because I couldn't wait to see you. I know things have been hard. We've been fighting and I wanted to come back and tell you that I can love you better. This is the longest we've been apart in months. I told you the time I'd be back. You said you'd see me then. Then, nothing! No note. No responses to texts. You don't answer your goddamn phone. When I finally hear from you, you don't even bother to tell me where you are. You just asked me to find you, and your friends, drugs. Then I come down here and you're with someone who's shooting up!"

"Do you even know me?" he exploded back. "How dare you accuse me of using! You don't know me at all. My phone died, okay? My phone died. Jesus fucking Christ!" He roared at me, face contorted.

We volleyed back and forth at full volume, our bodies wracked with the passion of our dispute. We'd face off then fling ourselves away. He stepped in my direction and I noticed a man, in his mid-forties, lingering on the path to my right. He stood on high alert. I knew instinctively that he was not staring at our train wreck of an argument out of morbid curiosity. He'd become my self-appointed watchman.

It's odd, to say the least, when the person for whom you leave love notes on the kitchen table, the one who comes looking for you reading in the living room if he wakes to find he can't wrap himself around you, flips some mental switch and can't compute that his sudden and complete absence is both terrifying and hurtful. It was downright surreal to notice, even amidst the collision of our two trains of tempers, that someone else was standing in vigilance, waiting to intercede if the person I loved most on the entire planet hit me. Apparently, our screaming match suggested domestic violence.

It was the watchman, with his alert eyes and rigid body that made me think, "I can't believe this is my life right now. When did this happen?"

This wasn't my character. This drama didn't even feel like my life, but it was. I switched gears. No one was giving an inch, and this couldn't go on. I shoved my way past him instead. "I can't do this anymore. Did you put in our notice at the apartment?" Oh yeah, we'd just bought an RV together. Classic Anika.

"No." he said, finally dropping a notch below full volume. I kept walking and made my way to the worn wooden staircase that led up to the road. I felt exasperated, broken, and tired. The lack of follow through was so small in comparison, yet still somehow symbolic.

I started up the stairs, then dared, "Why not?"

It wasn't until I reached the top that he shouted up after me. "I didn't think you were really in this."

"Jay, I was in it until right now."

This was not the true end. It never is. It was the beginning of the end. Perhaps more accurately the beginning of when I KNEW it was the end. I came home and put my back to the wall. I slid down it into a sobbing heap. I called upon all my friends. I howled with grief. I listened to a book on codependency. At one point, I begged, literally begged, on my hands and knees for my greatest love to get sober.

"Just give me thirty days." I pleaded. "If you love me, give me thirty days." I knew the answer before he gave it. I'd always known the answer. Yet I had to ask. I'd stubbornly squeezed shut my eyes but the fire of the truth still danced across my eyelids. The searing irrepressible reality I'd sensed from the beginning now blazed before my open eyes. Jay was, and always had been an alcoholic. From the very beginning, from our first encounter. I'd always known.

How in the heck, you may be wondering, does this apply to Intuition... especially after my confession to ignoring the deeply known? One of my favorite poets, Buddy Wakefield, speaks of this self-betrayal in his poem, "Hurling Crowbirds at Mockingjays." He bashfully explains, "all my eggs were in a basket of red flags." They were indeed. Most of my friends expressed as much. I could perceive their judgement and reticence even if they didn't. No one thought this was a good match for me. My love wore his trauma like a "beware of dog" sign. Falling in love with him was like riding a blatantly poorly constructed roller coaster.

If I got in my car alone, my mind would yell to me, "Run! Run! It's too scary!" but then I would feel into the deep well of my chest and my heart would say something else. It would coo softly, "Courage, Dear One. Here in the warm place, we are not scared. We do not care what the others think. We go towards love. Always."

My chest claimed I'd be okay. My heart let me fall in the love with that broken little boy. It held me while I held him when his dad died the same day I landed in Tacoma. It called me to leave my home and drive for months with my partner in crime, then ached when the time arrived to return back home to San Diego and my family of hoodlums. It told me to love and love and love and love some more. Then, it broke me.

I digress again, as is the nature of Tarantino style storytelling, but my point, dear friend, is not that I should have listened to my comrades and sidestepped this love hurricane. No, my point is that Intuition, often, dare I say, frequently runs us headfirst into pain. It can take you not only into "run of the mill" pain... but searing, screaming matches over heroin needles, strangers holding vigil, I'm so broken, I need all the help I can get, alert the doctor, call the therapist, track down an exorcist, bring in the shaman, I'm so fucked, feels like I'll never be unfucked, kinda pain.

To this day, I don't know if Jay ever got sober. Someone else did, however. Me. The courageous cowgirl in the center of my chest landed me on the back of a bucking bronco. It was the roughest, most exhilarating, most passionate, most gut-wrenching ride I've ever encountered. When I finally let his rage and recklessness toss me, you can be certain, I landed smack dab in a heaping mound of my own bullshit. You could smell the hypocrisy.

Here I was, begging someone to go thirty days without a drink, when I could count on one hand the number of times in the past year, I'd managed to stay dry for twenty-four hours. It took me nine months and A MIRACLE to pull off thirty days. On day twenty-six, while I sat in my room watching my hands shake and feeling like every emotion, I'd ever experienced had been lit on fire inside of my own body, my denial finally abated and I thought, "Holy shit. I'm an alcoholic."

Not maybe. Not, "perhaps I have a drinking problem." Not, I really need to "handle my drinking" No. This thing was out of my control. This was the reason I'd dated an alcoholic. THIS was the cause of my greatest suffering.

I've heard it said that we conjure up exactly the amount of pain necessary to motivate our own transformation. For me that amount of pain was losing who I thought was the love of my life to addiction. This pain forced me to examine my own behaviors in a new light, specifically one of those ominous and painfully bright lamps they use in interrogation rooms on television. It illuminated my addictions and my pattern of experiencing another person's pain as my own. I'd been hand-picking other alcoholics to be my closest companions. I'd select the shameless brand, the ones so far down the line, they started early and continued into the night. I'd pick the ones who made me feel better about myself, the ones that drank more than me, then I'd proceed to drink just a little bit less, so I could judge them and justify my own drinking. I could barely see over the heaps of bullshit and I felt like I was digging my way out with a popsicle stick.

Luckily, starting a twelve-step program felt like being handed a spade. Hearing voices outside the pile of my own crap offering stories about their own shit show made me feel less horrendous. I wasn't alone in my ass-holery. My comrades offered little nuggets of advice. They had a plan. It sounded ridiculous and rigid, but I was just desperate enough to try anything, and now here I sit, writing of sobriety. It was the exorcism for which I'd prayed for years. Oh, sweet desperation, ironically, you are a beautiful thing. In addition to my sobriety from alcohol, this love, this pain gave me one more incredible gift. I became less afraid of death. If I die tomorrow, I loved at least one human being with every inch of passion available to this body and this heart. I'd loved like a forest fire. I'd learned that I could. Since I believe love and learning to be the reigning "whys" behind being alive on this planet, diving into that very thing has helped me feel more prepared to leave it.

So, yes, all my eggs were in a basket of red flags, and yes, my eggs and I got crushed. I ended up all runny yolks and a crunchy, fragile pieces of shell. Thank goodness! Intuition doesn't always take us into the sweetness right away. It doesn't always lead us down the easiest path. Sometimes it takes us to freedom through breaking us down, completely. Sometimes it curls us into a ball of ache, before it delivers us beyond our begging. Sometimes it makes us wait and wait and wait like the slow click of a roller coaster reaching its peak before it takes us on the ride of our lifetime. Sometimes it says yes when the wisdom of people who love us and every aspect of reason says to run.

So tell me, tell me of your pain. Tell me of your ache. Tell me what broke you. Then tell me how you have or how you plan to rise. How has Intuition guided your transformation? Include how it took you in as well as how it got you out. Let's explore.

THE WORK

Explain an episode in which you willingly entered into a challenge:

List the thoughts, emotions, and experiences that caused you to pursue this challenge:

What was the outcome? What lessons were harvested during and in the aftermath of this experience?

Explain an episode in which you willingly entered into a challenge:

List the thoughts, emotions, and experiences that caused you to pursue this challenge:

What was the outcome? What lessons were harvested during and in the aftermath?

Perhaps you've encountered a less inspired incarnation of challenge. Let's refer to challenge's less intuitive sibling (though still, in his own way useful) as struggle.

Write the saga of a time you forced yourself to struggle.

What elements of emotion and/or lines of thinking affected your decision to stay in or enter into struggle? What feedback came from the body during this time?

What was the outcome of this struggle?

Write the saga of a time you forced yourself to struggle.

What elements of emotion and/or lines of thinking affected your decision to stay in or enter into struggle? What feedback came from the body during this time?

What was the outcome of this struggle?

Write the saga of a time you forced yourself to struggle.

What elements of emotion and/or lines of thinking affected your decision to stay in or enter into struggle? What feedback came from the body during this time?

What was the outcome of this struggle?

Pain is a necessary and inescapable part of life. At times, it may feel meaningless and unjust. It also purifies and propels us forward. I would argue that suffering is self-created. It holds us hostage. It is also a part of life. The last thing we need when we are suffering is someone to shame us for it. I'm not here to shame you. I don't advocate for self-scourging, but if you're willing to examine the thoughts and feelings around the instances and eras you've chosen to suffer, you might be able to call in just enough pain (or bliss) to get yourself out of suffering.

Outline an instance, week, month, or entire era of life in which you suffered.

What motivated this suffering? What were your views about the world and yourself at this time? List a few frequent thoughts you had during or immediately preceding this period. Recall any belief systems to which you ascribed. What prominent behaviors or behavior patterns defined this era?

What expectations did you have of yourself during this period? What expectations did you have of others? What did you expect from life?

Has this suffering ended? If so, extrapolate on the catalyst that caused this change. What beliefs or belief systems shifted? Which behaviors? What strategies were helpful in moving through and past this suffering? Who supported you through this change?

Outline an instance, week, month, or entire era of life in which you suffered.

What motivated this suffering? What were your views about the world and yourself at this time? List a few frequent thoughts you had during or immediately preceding this period. Recall any belief systems to which you ascribed. What prominent behaviors or behavior patterns defined this era?

What expectations did you have of yourself? What expectations did you have of others? What expectations did you have of life?

Has this suffering ended? If so, extrapolate on the catalyst that caused this change. What beliefs or belief systems shifted? Which behaviors? What strategies were helpful in moving through and past this suffering? Who supported you through this change?

In contrast, let's examine pain.

Depict a point in which your heart, your courageousness, or life itself led you into pain.

How did you feel in your body, mind, and heart before you were blindsided by this pain? How did you feel during? After?

What did pain teach you? Specify the lessons you extracted during or in the aftermath of this run-in with pain?

Depict a point in which your heart, your courageousness, or life itself led you into pain.

How did you feel in your body, mind, and heart before you were blindsided by this pain?

What did pain teach you? Specify the lessons you extracted during or in the aftermath of this run-in with pain?

Let's compare and contrast.

What were the most distinctive differences that surfaced between what motivated you towards a challenge versus towards a struggle? How do these experiences differ in emotional and physical experience? Define the distinctive differences between their outcomes.

What did you discover to be the distinction between what motivated you towards pain versus suffering? How do these experiences differ in emotional and physical experience? Define the distinctive differences between their outcomes.

Record the biggest takeaways or any additional insights:

I commonly prescribe the exercise below to students and clients dealing with physical pain, but, I find it to be helpful with emotional turmoil as well. Odds are that pain is present in your life **RIGHT NOW** in some form or the other. In the space below, compose a letter to yourself from your pain. It might be helpful to clear your mind with a few minutes of soft (or hard core) meditation. Give yourself permission to feel what you need to feel and to speak for your own personal pain.

Dear——————,

Hello, I am your pain. Here is what I have to tell you.

With love,

~ Your Pain

I told the story of one of my darkest hours. I believe in that very hour a germinating strength cracked its seedy casing and sent out the tentacle of tenacity that now bears the fruit of one of my greatest triumphs. Speak to me of triumph!

Tell the tale of one your greatest triumphs:

What were some of the catalysts or motivations for pursuing this change or endeavor?

Expound on what you overcame or transcended in order to accomplish this undertaking.

What were the feelings that surrounded this triumph? What emotions do you currently associate with it?

Tell the tale of one of your greatest triumphs:

What were some of the catalysts or motivations for pursuing this change or endeavor?

Expound on what you overcame or transcended in order to accomplish this undertaking.

What feelings surrounded this triumph? What emotions do you currently associate with it?

Tell the tale of one of your greatest triumphs:

What were some of the catalysts or motivations for pursuing this change or endeavor?

Expound on what you overcame or transcended in order to accomplish this undertaking.

How do you feel in regard to this triumph?

SECTION 4:
MERGE WITH MYSTERY

"If you can align yourself with what wants to happen, things will be done through you that you cannot do yourself."

-Martha Beck

The talented teacher, musician, and borderline magician, Josh Brill, once granted me the gift of a guitar lesson. He began with a conversational lecture by illustrating how music is built on mathematical principles. We discussed the science of our emotional bodies and their reactions when musical frequencies greet our physical form. His description of music blended the practical with the profound, as though the two things could not be extricated from one another. Perhaps this is true. It rang as awesome to me. He proceeded to guide me through playing one note, by strumming one string, and refraining from playing again until after I had heard and felt the note complete its bouncing, vibrating journey of ending. I closed my eyes and spent a few minutes feeling my chest and arms resting on the wooden body of the instrument. I sensed my fingers softly inviting the string to express itself. I listened for the death of the vibration I'd encouraged into being. Then he gave me another instruction.

"Now, wait to play the string until you hear or feel that the note wants to be played." This instruction metaphorically represented an overall shift that was saturating the way I approached the entirety of my life. I'd been utilizing a metric ton of effort to try to "create the life of my dreams" when it felt immensely better to flow with life on life's terms. Life and music are both ruled by the same mathematical principles. My subjective experience supports that when I get a little hollow, or at least get out of my own way and stop orchestrating everything to be as I believe it should be, this miraculous symphony of life unfolds harmoniously.

Artists tend to understand this. They become channels for their medium rather than creators. Talented teachers speak of the same sensation. Some fantastic writers reminisce of an insight arriving through them rather than from them. There is no portion on this process of surrendering to what wants to happen that is harder for me personally than opening up the timeline. Patience is not among my natural virtues. Truth be told, timing is beyond me. Despite my best efforts and ridiculous antics, I've never had the final say.

THE WORK

Since we're exploring the path of the artist, find a set of crayons, coloured pencils, or markers. In the space below, compose a good old-fashioned doodle: draw whatever YOU want!

Now staying connected with the same experience of your own preferences, colour in the shapes below. Feel free to use the space around the shapes as you see fit.

On this page, begin by feeling into the shapes themselves. How do these shapes want to be coloured? Close your eyes, feel the texture of your utensil. Note how you hold it. How does the tool you've chosen desire to move? Sense the surface of the paper. How does the paper want to engage with your hand, the air, the crayon or pencil? Instead of focusing on you and your desires, sense what wants to happen and play along. Use the space below to bring your perception of what the shapes want to be to life.

Try doodling again or creating out of thin air. First feel into your body, sense the utensil in your hand, perceive or imagine how the page wants to be left open or filled. Now begin.

What was the difference in how you felt during these colouring exercises?

Examine the two expressions of colour inside of shape. How do you feel towards the outcome of these two pieces? Did the container of the shapes make this easier or more difficult?

Examine your doodles, sketches, or expressions of colour. How do you feel towards the outcome of these two pieces?

Who gives a fuck? How is this pertinent to you and the way you navigate your life currently? Write your insights below.

It's entirely possible that when you were asked to "feel into what wants to happen," your mind, in its obstinacy, remained obnoxiously blank. This happened to me often when I was nineteen and expected to pick a major in college. It felt like an unmanned fire hose was whipping around at full blast in my brain, pistol whipping my amygdala and dousing my ability to determine my own desires. It wasn't uncommon for me to land myself in a mental tailspin that ended in tears and prayers.

"Please, God!" I'd beg, "Help me to know what to do with my life!" As I mentioned earlier, patience and/or surrendering to divine timing (or the timing of anyone else for that matter) has never been my strong suit. It never crossed my worried, nineteen-year-old brain that perhaps it was okay to not be certain of my life's direction at this tender age (or any age, really). I couldn't have fathomed that uncertainty would be an inescapable life companion, let alone that it'd be riding shotgun every time I let the powerful pull of my heart's delight steer this vessel.

If you are metaphorically ready to pull your hair out over choosing your major or brought to tears at your own incapability to make a simple decision, you're not alone. If you're desperate for answers, but in all truthfulness, not certain how to answer the question: "what wants to happen?" Let alone, "what does my heart say?" There's no need to toss the gasoline of guilt onto the embers of frustration.

Sensing what wants to take place is a very advanced expression of interpreting your own intuitive language. It requires identifying subtlety and being willing to vocalize and even act on small or silly impressions. It also stems from the decision to consciously activate your intuitive mind. If you currently don't feel you have the ability to make impromptu intuitive contact, fear not, my friend! Intuition finds you. Gird your loins! Keep your eyes peeled! If you look for it, it will find you. Insight is coming.

SECTION 5:
RADICAL ROCK PILES

"In order to find the treasure, you'll have to follow the omens."

Paulo Coelho - The Alchemist

If you've been on many hikes, you may be familiar with "trail code." Trail code outlines the agreed upon rules that most hiker's adhere to in consideration of others, such as: not blasting music, letting the person who is hiking uphill keep their stride by stepping aside, packing out everything you brought with you, etc. There is also a code to how the trail is marked. For instance, it's common to see stones stacked on top of one another as a way to mark the trail if you're traversing rocky terrain. Branches are strategically placed in front of deceptively trail-like paths that lead into brush or cacti. These are examples of trail markers. They're not as explicit as a sign post pounded into the earth, but once you're aware of these slightly more subtle methods of communication, you have the option to allow them to direct your next steps. Moving from trail marker to trail marker commonly leads to enchanted forests, personal triumphs, and gorgeous summits that were invisible or daunting from the vantage point of the trailhead.

Here are some common trail markers:

Coincidence:

Carl Jung is credited for coining the term "synchronicity" also known as "meaningful coincidences." A coincidence often smells of Intuition, but if you are experiencing a string of back to back coincidences, well then, breath deep and follow that scent like a bloodhound, because you're onto something.

At the beginning of 2017, I looked at my vision for the year and realized that everything on the list read uninspired and reachable. I'd erred on the side of "attainable" and plotted a path towards "boring and safe." I pulled out a scratch piece of paper and wrote on the top, "Dream 2017" and began to feverishly scribble impossible ideas. I kept nothing off the list and instead tried to focus on what I would do if limitations vanished. In the end, a note card with the word "Europe" got pasted onto the dream board.

It was not in the budget. I hadn't been abroad in years. It seemed like an irresponsible pipe dream and Europe seemed like the least likely continent, given it was also the most expensive. The previous fall, I'd been foiled in my attempt to register for a training in Spain, but had taken to stalking the website, in case, perchance, a space became available in the training that would validate my European excursion.

As fate would have it, one month before the training, after I'd given up on the idea completely, purchased other trainings, and solidified plans to vacation with friends in other locations, I made my now habitual sweep of the website. The words "One space available!" sparkled at me beside the Spain listing. I floated on waves of surrealism. In the tangible world, I feverishly emailed my interest. I checked on flights to every airport in Spain and Portugal, all of which exceeded a thousand dollars.

The replying email informed me that another person had responded more quickly than I. I'd be the first to know if the individual declined the opportunity. They assured me the person would confirm by the end of the week. A week passed. No email. Another week passed. No email. Then, like trumpets blasting from fluffy, animated clouds, (think Monty Python and the Search for the Holy Grail) an email finally arrived announcing my acceptance to the Spain training module. With equal fanfare, Air France suddenly decided to allow me to fly to from San Diego to Madrid for a mere four hundred dollars!

This deal suddenly appeared the day of my acceptance into the program. Four hundred dollars! As though my fairy Godmother had popped into my bedroom, yelled, "Bippity Boppity, Boo-yah!" (my fairy Godmother would!) and transformed my Priceline feed with the wave of her magical wand. It was the perfect storm of coincidences. It was straight serendipity. It was the gravitational pull that is all things coalescing to provide clear and undeniable direction. It all clicked like my spine cracking at the chiropractor.

Now let's look at some of your single serving or strings of coincidences. If you don't have a vivid recent memory of a coincidence or group of coincidences, you may want to wait until you have one. Don't worry, your brain will already be on high alert for such happenings. You won't have to wait long.

THE WORK

Lay out the particulars of your most recently experienced coincidence (single serving):

What, if any, meaning did you assign to this coincidence?

Lay out the particulars of a memorable or recently experienced coincidence (single serving):

What, if any, meaning did you assign to this coincidence?

Lay out the particulars of a memorable or recently experienced coincidence (single serving):

What, if any, meaning did you assign to this coincidence?

TALKING TO TRUTH

Paraphrase your most recent bout of synchronicity or string of coincidences:

Outline your relationship to time during the occurrence of these coincidences (Did it all seem to happen at once? Did it arrive in the nick of time? Did time stand still?) :

What did this synchronicity mean to/for you?

Paraphrase a memorable or recent bout of synchronicity or string of coincidences:

Outline your relationship to time during the occurrence of these coincidences (Did it all seem to happen at once? Did it arrive in the nick of time? Did time stand still?) :

What did this synchronicity mean to/for you?

Paraphrase a memorable or recent bout of synchronicity or string of coincidences:

Outline your relationship to time during the occurrence of these coincidences. (Did it all seem to happen at once? Did it arrive in the nick of time? Did time stand still?):

What meaning do you attribute to this synchronicity?

Note any expectations or desires that may have coloured your interpretation of both your single servings coincidences or synchronicities:

Omens

When the notorious boyfriend and I took a two-month lap around the country, he asked a friend to fly to Washington state and drive with us. We packed Spartacus, the intrepid silver Corolla to her rooftop and welcomed our fellow explorer. In exchange, she delivered the crowning jewel of our adventure, The Road Trip Game. Essentially it was a game her father developed with the purpose of keeping his precocious child occupied during road trips under the guise of teaching her math skills. I imagine the man to be both bored and brilliant, a combination that tends to lead to one of two things: creation or destruction. Praise be unto the Car Gods that he chose creation. Since Spartacus had not simply been stuffed with the possessions of three people but also their semi-problematic egos and borderline obsessive competitive drives, The Game quickly became the meaning of our road trip existence.

The rules to The Game (as played by us) are as follows:

A player receives five points for being the first one to correctly call and identify: a Volkswagen bug or a taxi.

If any claim proves false, the amount of points normally allocated for the claim are instead deducted from the players score.

A player receives ten points each time they are the first person in the vehicle to verbally acknowledge a limousine, a police car, or a "beaver." Any vehicle sporting wood paneling is considered a "beaver."

A player may score by successfully locating a "trash bag window" which is not limited to trash bags. Other acceptable (and seen) variations might include: a duct taped window, a cardboard window, a tarped window, or a window constructed entirely of cereal boxes. Basically, if your car window is broken and rather than taking it to a window professional, you've elected to deflect the elements and possible theft with the use of a low cost, flimsy, and potentially creative alternative, you are the proud or less than proud owner of a trash bag window. Your vehicle is worth twenty-five points in the greatest car game of all car games. The record currently states Cleveland, Ohio to be the city with the highest number of trash bag windows per capita.

A majestic hawk sighting secures a player fifty points.

The game ends when the first player reaches one hundred points. The same player who reaches a hundred points surrenders their crown, falls from grace and power, and receives the title of ultimate loser if they engage in any sort of celebration or gloating following their victory. My first three triumphs slipped through my celebrating jazz hands due to my charming and deeply entrenched tendency to rub my own excellence in other people's faces.

There is one elusive entity that is worth the entire one hundred points and thus wins a player The Game. This is known as "The Golden Beaver." The Golden Beaver is a PT Cruiser with wood paneling. It is an absurd vehicle that no practical person would ever purchase, and yet, it exists. (if you own one, please write to me and explain yourself!) The Golden Beaver heralds as the laurel wreath of The Car Game.

After spending hours and hours scanning roadways for a glistening PT Cruiser with its iconic stripe of faux wood, I still gasp when one rolls past me or appears in an unassuming driveway. For a period of time, after the explosion that was the end of the relationship, the sight of the game-winning beaver filled me with fury, then sadness. Today, it's matured into a symbol of luck, good fortune, and a memo to me that I'm moving towards magic. The Golden Beaver morphed into a beacon of hope and an indicator that the person or events at hand will play a significant role in the plotline of my life.

Others have shared that a set of numbers appearing in front of their eyes feels like a message from a deceased loved one. I consider déjà vu to be a surreal radar for scouting my heart's path. The sound or sight of certain animals are often considered auspicious. Whatever symbol you ascribe to doesn't really matter, it becomes potent in its meaning to you personally.

Perhaps omens appear because we want them to appear, replicating magical realism in our sometimes lackluster lives. A relevant question regarding your own use or belief in omens might be, "Does it benefit you?" Do omens strike alongside recklessness? Does it coincide with a sense of despair? Or, is it possible your omens relay messages of peace, forgiveness, love, hope, validation, and direction? Call me idealistic, but if omens enhance your life and fill you with well-being, then I don't give a flying frankfurter whether it's the placebo effect or the omen itself. In my experience, believing in and looking for the magic inside of this reality creates a mental gateway for seeing and feeling it everywhere.

Let's see if we can home in on some your own personal omens!

THE WORK

List any sights, scents, patterns, icons, animals, or people with which you have strong affiliations. Enumerate your past of current personal omens. Whittle down this list (or inflate it with some guesswork, depending) to entities and icons that cultivate feelings of peace, hope, exuberance, or otherwise exhibit "omen potential."

When was the last time you had a visceral or emotional reaction to one of these messengers? Explain the experience in detail. Where were you? What were you doing? What struck you most about this sighting or encounter?

What meaning or interpretation did you ascribe to this experience? How did you feel? Did any words register? How, if at all, did this affect your next course of action?

Let's try this again. If you answered the questions for an omen with which you have a strong sense of connection, this time answer the questions with regard to a messenger with which your connection seems vague. Observe the differences in the quality of the experience when you've encountered this entity. There's no need to judge or force it. Repeat this exercise for all your potential omens. You may discover that you have more omens than you originally realized. If you have a plethora of potential omens, you may want to continue this exercise in your journal or on a separate piece of paper.

When was the last time you had a visceral or emotional reaction to one of these messengers? Elaborate on the details. Where were you? What were you doing? What struck you most about this sighting or encounter?

What meaning or interpretation did you ascribe to this experience? How did you feel? Did any words register? How, if at all, did this affect your next course of action?

When was the last time you had a visceral or emotional reaction to one of these messengers? Elaborate on the details. Where were you? What were you doing? What struck you most about this sighting or encounter?

What meaning or interpretation did you ascribe to this experience? How did you feel? Did any words register? How, if at all, did this affect your next course of action?

When was the last time you had a visceral or emotional reaction to one of these messengers? Elaborate on the details. Where were you? What were you doing? What struck you most about this sighting or encounter?

What meaning or interpretation did you ascribe to this experience? How did you feel? Did any words register? How, if at all, did this affect your next course of action?

Now let's use what you've written about your experience with omens to unveil your personal truth. It's commonly said that the cream rises to the top. Perhaps it could also be said (less delicately) that a good, healthy, fully-digested bowel movement sinks right to the bottom. (I'm only a little sorry.)

I like this metaphor for a few reasons. Firstly, learning to speak your own intuitive language, much like everything else, requires a good amount of time utilizing the process of elimination. I like to keep in mind that simply because something doesn't speak to me any longer doesn't discredit its helpfulness in the past. Furthermore, this entity, like the Golden Beaver, could transform from a confusing caterpillar to a vibrant beacon of a butterfly with time.

When we are grieving, we look everywhere for meaning. When we are lost, every street sign, vaguely familiar rock formation, stranger walking purposefully, or tarp flapping in the wind becomes a life line or a puzzle piece. If it helps you, gives you a lick of comfort, somehow makes it easier to put one foot in front of the other, or inspires the rising flutter of hope, I say keep it... until it doesn't. If it stops working for you, if it seems old and raggedy, if it wafts of desperation, or if it simply muddies the waters of your clarity to see an omen every time its 3:33, then honey, flush that shit.

Which, if any, of your potential omens hang ripe for elimination or composting?

Why? Describe the quality or the feelings around these patterns or entities. Did these omens lose their potency over time or shift with your perspective? When did you notice these changes? Was there wishful thinking?

Take inventory of the entities, objects, sounds, numbers, or feelings you believe to be your current personal omens.

What do these omens have in common? Is there a unifying theme between them? How did you identify them?

SECTION 6:
BODACIOUS BOOKS AND BAD-ASS TEACHERS

"Some books make us free."

– Ralph Waldo Emerson

"Never trust anyone who has not brought a book with them."

– Lemony Snicket

Have the words of a friend or teacher ever rained on you with all the refreshment of a waterfall? Have you ever read a few lines from a page and gasped at the sheer veracity of it all? Our non-verbal experience can alert us when a soul shaking truth crosses our awareness. Your body may send you a signal or your mind could snap into alertness. The words might taste so real and touch a place so raw that you could have written them with your own hand or spoken them from your own lips. Odds are, if you're running around waving your arms having what Oprah refers to as an "a-ha moment," you're probably receiving communication from your Intuition.

What's nice about written word and living teachers is that it cuts out the sometimes stumble-y business of interpretation. The meaning stands directly in front of you. All you have to do is note its importance and scratch the words into your heart, and let the sweet scars of this truth shape you as you move forward. Sounds simple, right?

This moves us into stage two of learning to speak your intuitive language: accountability. How will you use your gift of fresh comprehension and understanding? How do you move from apt interpretation into, first graceless, then deft application? It all starts with paying attention. Then, it converges into a willingness to fail miserably, brave uncertainty, and look like a Godforsaken idiot. Finally, it focalizes into a long term, committed, and loving relationship with your passions and insights, even in times when you are facing the dark night of the soul. (Dammit! Again?) Clearly, this will take some practice.

Let's investigate! If you've received recent insights, hand delivered to you by a loving conversation with a friend or your latest read, feel free to examine them. You might also pull from memory and reference iconic teachers or literature that have heavily influenced you or splashed you with the cold water that shocked you into changing your life. If nothing comes to mind, you can wait. Set your intention to receive an insight and listen with new ears for the sound of sage advice. Pick up a piece of literature that's aimed to inspire and see what jumps off the page and attacks your face or whispers soft, gentle truths.

THE WORK

Write out your most recently discovered insight. This may have been delivered through the mouth of a loved one, a teacher, or through a form of media such as film, podcasts, videos, or literature.

Characterize your feelings when you encountered this insight. Why did it stand out to you? Factor in timing. Did this insight speak to your experience in the past, present, or future? Would a previous version of you have understood this message?

Rewrite the insight in your own words below.

Write out a recent or memorable insight that came from an outside source. This may have been delivered through the mouth of a loved one, a teacher, or through a form of media such as film, podcasts, videos, or literature.

Characterize your feelings when you encountered this insight. Why did it stand out to you? Factor in timing.

Rewrite the insight in your own words below.

Write out a recent or memorable insight that came from an outside source. This may have been delivered through the mouth of a loved one, a teacher, or through a form of media such as film, podcast, video, or literature.

Characterize your feelings when you encountered this insight. Why did it stand out to you? Factor in timing.

Rewrite the insight in your own words below.

Great! You've outlined some hand-delivered messages from your Intuition. Now, my sweet one, you graduate to the application!

How, if at all, have these insights affected you and your life? Did they shift your attitude and if so, in what way? How has each insight shaped your behavior?

Close your eyes and imagine that you knew, felt, and understood the listed insights to be true in every cell of your body. Imagine your "rewrites" are being etched into your heart. How would it feel to move through the world from this place of powerful knowing? (Pretend, if need be)

Write yourself an action plan! List five to ten ideas for integrating these insights into your actions and encounters. If you already live your day to day life in compete trust of these insights, how can you deepen your commitment? Just like you may adore a loved one and still benefit from writing a small list or plan as to how you might show them this love more fully, you can affirm your love to your Intuition by honouring her insights. As you make your action plan, you are encouraged to make your to do list measurable, attainable, and also decidedly different or beyond your normal course of action. This to do list should stimulate similar sensations as the ones you felt when you wrote your insights on your heart. If the action plan seems like a drag, bag it. Write a list that speaks to your soul instead. Fuck shoulds.

Commit. Do it. Follow through. Live from this intuitive intent. Then, after a predetermined amount of time, write about it below!

What the hell happened!?!?!?!

SECTION 7:
PASS THE PEACE PIPE!

"Forgiveness is for anyone who needs a safe passage through their mind."

- Buddy Wakefield

While the campfire danced shadows on the faces of my new-found friends, I shot a glance at Jamie, our contractor and fearless leader. He frequently displayed a fractured and luminous heart whenever I asked a probing question. I inquired,

"Jamie, what was the best day of your life?" Jamie and his father, as mortals, had a complicated relationship. His father went into recovery from alcoholism during Jamie's adolescence. Baseball, whether as a conversation piece or an activity, always made his Dad's eyes shine.

In boyhood and beyond, Jamie and his Dad shared this pastime. They could come home to its simplicity when the complexities of their relationship seemed to scream. Jamie's father was diagnosed with terminal cancer. A month before he passed away, Jamie and his Dad went to the field a final time to hit a few balls. Jamie flicked a glance my way, cleared his throat, then stared back into the fire as he shared this bittersweet snippet.

"Every pitch my Dad threw zipped down the middle, and every ball I hit soared into the outfield. He'd never pitched so well, and I'd never hit so far. We both knew what it meant. We cried for joy at our perfect game of baseball, but also for coming home to our passion and to each other a final time before our last goodbye" His story set the stage for a unique set of answers to a question I'd asked many times. The next thing I knew the spotlight of flickering flames was shifting around the fire as each person shared their most MEANINGFUL day.

A gentleman across the ring of dancing light shared the story of an answered prayer. A lifetime of shame and remorse had brought him to his knees, an option unfathomable until someone stingingly suggested he had nowhere else to go. His life had lost all meaning. His body had become a cage and he was rapidly fading away. So try it, he did. He said he told the Man, the Woman, the Force, the Energy, the Universe, the Something, the Anything behind the curtain, everything he'd done. He said he didn't

166

know how he could be forgiven. He asked how he could possibly go on. He asked how to fix it, how to bear it, how to make it okay.

For the first time something answered. Suddenly, he was washed with warmth and the grief lifted. The strong, steady thought arrived in his mind.

"Don't worry about that today." a voice said. It's said the same thing every day since. It cradles his guilt and kindly reminds him "Lay your shame and your worry here, I'll hold it for you. Today you go out and do the best you can. We'll worry about the rest of it tomorrow."

"Lay down your burdens" the voice instructed. Essentially those same words arrive in the nick of time to each and every one of us. Every person I know has a story just like this one. I, myself, cherish a handful. Sometimes, all we get is peace of mind. We don't get lightning or a new life, at least, not in one sitting. We often feel a little new once we empty ourselves. It's a little easier to do the work of building after we set down that big bag of rocks we've been toting around with us.

"Don't worry about that today." said the voice, and that little tip changed the life of the man that sat across the fire.

If you feel currently any of those hip words like peaceful, centered, or content, odds are you've been listening to your intuitive guidance. If you are suffering immensely and a warm, soothing sensation rushes into your body and mind, that's Intuition as well. You

167

don't have to feel okay right this second in order to know you'll be okay in the future. It's considered a sign of one who is connected to their own inner insight to be able to maintain a sense of stillness even when crossing paths with challenge, hardship, or life's injustice.

You could take it a step further. When deciding a course of action, contemplate how the thought of each option makes you feel. Does this give you a sense of contentment? Exhilaration? Relief? Go that way. Does the option fill you with dread, disgust, entrapment, anger, or frustration? Perhaps this isn't your personal path. Let your decisions feel good.

This doesn't mean you'll never make a hard choice. Nor does it mean you'll never take the excruciating steps away from something or someone you love, crave, or whose absence is unimaginable. Your Intuition doesn't want you to be miserable, even if you embrace misery for a time in order to set yourself free. Take if from an alcoholic, sometimes following the intuitive guidance that gets you out of a shitty situation is horrifically uncomfortable... the only thing worse being to ignore the guidance and remain stagnant.

Sometimes Intuition strikes by placing a powerful book in our hands just when we're ready to read and absorb its message. Sometimes a person we love asks us a pertinent question. Sometimes a person we loathe shines a light on an aspect of ourselves we've avoided addressing. Sometimes romance or friendship or a colleague presents us with an opportunity to learn in an unexpected way.

If you start paying attention, if you utilize the skills you've been cultivating in stillness and observation, you'll start to notice the wiggly feeling in your belly or the prickle on your back that indicates these words, or questions, or interactions could be meaningful. You might even find they are all meaningful.

For me, when someone uses beautiful words that touch my heart, I get goosebumps and the hairs on my arms stand up. This also might happen when a powerful speaker enters the room. If someone asks me a question that touches the root of an issue I'm not excited to face, I get a rush of impatience and tend to want to lash out, flee, or close the conversation. I might even get nauseous. Through therapy and a strong desire not to behave like my father, I've learned to lean into this discomfort more frequently. Lord knows I still try to abandon ship. After testing this reaction a few times, I've come to learn that this discomfort usually indicates that friction is required to scrub the burnt honey off the frying pan of my soul.

Your body, feelings, and perhaps your mental and verbal insights are constantly alerting you when something around you requires your attention. All you have to do is watch those responses and learn how to interpret them. It's not so hard to home in on what's real, at least it won't be if you allow yourself to make mistakes. If you are tough on yourself for misinterpreting or missing these cues all together, then you will miss much. Your perfectionism will make this process more painful and increase the likelihood of giving up. So instead, try to err, aim to see your Intuition everywhere and when you flip-flop reality and fantasy, have yourself a good laugh, take lots of notes, and move on.

In the following exercise, let's focus on the experience of being with a person in their whole-ness or the entirety of your interaction with them or their work, rather than one specific statement or insight. In our previous exercise I might have relayed my experience with the words "thou mayest" appearing in the book East of Eden by John Steinbeck. In this exercise, I might relay an encounter of meeting John Steinbeck (in my dreams!) or how the book as a whole affected me. Feel free to use entirely different and unrelated examples!

THE WORK

Describe a recent or prominent memory in which you were moved or inspired by the words or presence of public speaker, friend, or acquaintance:

What were the physical and mental sensations that accompanied this experience? Did you pop out of reverie just in time to listen intently? Did goosebumps rise on your arms when the Dalai Lama entered the room? Did you feel calm or warm or exhilarated? Was your attention span longer than usual?

Boil down what you took away from this experience to just one concise sentence. How did this affect your life outside of the experience? How long did this affect or new belief last?

Describe a recent or prominent memory in which you were moved or inspired by the words or presence of public speaker, friend, or acquaintance:

What were the physical and mental sensations that accompanied this experience?

Boil down what you took away from this experience to just one concise sentence. How did this affect your life outside of the experience? How long did this affect or new belief last?

Describe a recent or prominent memory in which you were moved or inspired by the words or presence of public speaker, friend, or acquaintance:

What were the physical and mental sensations that accompanied this experience?

Boil down what you took away from this experience to just one concise sentence. How did this affect your life outside of the experience? How long did this effect or new belief last?

Now let's try it with what I call, "The Daddy Effect." Without getting too Freudian, let's assume that this is the shifty, icky, annoying discomfort that arises when there's an opportunity to choose to step out of our previous conditioning. This conditioning often runs deep, all the way back to mommy and daddy or perhaps beyond. It could also be a freshly woven net of overcompensation for the original pattern or an adaptation produced to protect an emotional or physical injury. The body, as a beautiful metaphor, displays this pattern of pain and protection. It's incredible that we can shift to accommodate injury while the body heals.

However, we'll continue to confront pain if we don't use the tools of modern understanding, awareness, and diligence in order to reestablish equilibrium. In order to fully heal, we must become willing to accept that this pattern of protection is no longer supportive of balance. Then, we must surrender the old way, and educate ourselves on how to strengthen the muscles that stopped participating fully. The discipline of full participation is often wrought with friction. It requires showing up in small doses. Sometimes, it necessitates doing less so you can play the long game. It requires squaring off with yourself and probing your own deficiencies. It asks you to choose this assessment on a daily basis, if can manage it. Then, (and this is important) loving yourself every single centimeter of the way!

"Friction feelings" might be the equivalent of a sidekick in a suspense film shouting from behind you, "It's a trap!" The snares of society and psychology can steal your freedoms. Your trusty sidekick isn't trying to punk you, he's ringing the liberty bell to signify an opportunity to claim your independence. I don't know anyone who enjoys the provocative sounds and high alert feelings associated with alarms, but damn if they aren't useful.

THE WORK

Note a recent or prominent instance in which you were being controlled by your conditioning or playing out an old protective pattern. (Of course, not all conditioning is maladaptive, but for the sake of this exercise, let's focus on examples when your conditioning hindered your ability to grow as an individual or experience joy.)

What "friction feelings" alerted you to this situation? Did pride or defensiveness burst out of you? Did you take feedback personally? Were you afraid of speaking up or standing out? Were you jealous, competitive, or desperate? Did guilt or shame surface? Was there grappling for control? Did you scan the room for exits or make plans to move?

Who or what did you blame? (Blame is HUGE, y'all! It gets its own section.)

In what ways did you or can you lovingly hold yourself accountable? How did you rumble with this conditioning? When did you shift your perspective or behavior? On a scale of one to ten, rate the difficulty of this shift?

Note a recent or prominent instance in which you became aware that you were being controlled by your conditioning or playing out an old protective pattern.

What "friction feelings" alerted you to this situation?

Who or what did you blame? (I reiterate, HUGE.)

In what ways did you or can you lovingly hold yourself accountable? How did you rumble with this conditioning? When did you shift your perspective or behavior? On a scale of one to ten, rate the difficulty of this shift?

Note a recent or prominent instance in which you became aware that you were being controlled by your conditioning or playing out an old protective pattern.

What "friction feelings" alerted you to this situation?

Who or what did you blame?

In what ways did you or can you lovingly hold yourself accountable? How did you rumble with this conditioning? When did you shift your perspective or behavior? On a scale of one to ten, rate the difficulty of this shift?

The gentleman across the fire spoke of being swaddled in the sweet serenity of peace. You might experience this as one sweeping and consuming moment, like when the mind stops spinning as you gaze at a sunset or when your slate gets wiped clean as you realize you're forgiven. It could be a state of being you embody for a period of time. Just as Super Mario swells with power and resiliency once he absorbs a bright red, polka-dotted mushroom, you too, expand and strengthen when you maintain contact with peace. Enlightenment, that elusive minx, might be defined as when the flickering flame of serenity steadies and shines with blissful stillness and consistent luminosity.

Paint yourself a word portrait of a powerful or recent blast of peace.

Expound on the details of your circumstance. Where were you? What were you doing? What company did you keep? Outline your emotional state before, during, and after peace rocked you to your core.

Formulate a sentence that embodies the sentiment of this serenity. Did peace serve as a guide post? Distinguish the direction it steered your course.

Paint yourself a word portrait of a powerful or recent blast of peace.

Expound on the details of your circumstance. Where were you? What were you doing? What company did you keep? Outline your emotional state before, during, and after peace rocked you to your core.

Formulate a sentence that embodies the sentiment of this serenity. Did peace serve as a guide post? Distinguish the direction it steered your course.

Paint yourself a word portrait of a powerful or recent blast of peace.

Expound on the details of your circumstance. Where were you? What were you doing? What company did you keep? Outline your emotional state before, during, and after peace rocked you to your core.

Formulate a sentence that embodies the sentiment of this serenity. Did peace serve as a guide post? Distinguish the direction it steered your course.

Depict an era of life when you felt consistently, steadily, or frequently connected to peace.

Expound on the details of your circumstance. What defined this time of life? Recall any prominent habits or practices. (Were you working out? Smoking the Ganja? Meditating? Soliciting strangers for sex? Taking walks on the beach? On or off coffee? Praying to the fertility Gods? Performing random acts of kindness?)

TALKING TO TRUTH

Give a brief synopsis of how you were meeting the following human needs. Estimate the amount of time and energy you were investing in each.

Physical Well-Being:

Purpose or Meaning:

Play and Pleasure:

Intimacy, Romance, and Friendship:

Autonomy, Self-Care, and Solitude:

Variety, Exploration, Growth, and Adventure:

Depict an era of life when you felt consistently, steadily, or frequently connected to peace.

Expound on the details of your circumstance. What defined this time of life? Recall any prominent habits or practices.

Give a brief synopsis of how you were meeting the following human needs. Estimate the amount of time and energy you were investing in each.

Physical Well-Being:

Purpose or Meaning:

Play and Pleasure:

Intimacy, Romance, and Friendship:

Autonomy, Self-Care, and Solitude:

Variety, Exploration, Growth, and Adventure:

Depict an era of life when you felt consistently, steadily, or frequently connected to peace.

Expound on the details of your circumstance. What defined this time of life? Recall any prominent habits or practices.

Give a brief synopsis of how you were meeting the following human needs. Estimate the amount of time and energy you were investing in each.

Physical Well-Being:

Purpose or Meaning:

Play and Pleasure:

Intimacy, Romance, and Friendship:

Autonomy, Self-Care, and Solitude:

Variety, Exploration, Growth, and Adventure:

Write an invitation to Peace. Invite her to the party that is your life or this particular era of it. Review the previous instances when peace played on your team. Sweeten the deal by stipulating how you plan to set the stage for her arrival. Just a like a great friend, verbalize your enjoyment and appreciation. Avoid making demands of peace. Give peace the same autonomy and empowerment you'd want for yourself.

Dear Peace,

You're Invited!

With love and gratitude,

SECTION 8:
NOCTURNAL VISITORS

"We have forgotten the age-old fact that God speaks chiefly through dreams and visions."

-Carl Jung

No book on Intuition would be complete without addressing the world of dreams. Oft-times our dreams reflect our anxieties. Sometimes they're just plain weird as fuck. Learning to speak your intuitive language requires that we learn to distinguish the meaningful from the meaningless. This is as true in the world of dreams as it is anywhere else.

You are the captain of your own intuitive ship. As captain it will be your task to read the waters, the stars, and the wind. Smooth sailing is more likely when you steer accordingly. Here are some suggestions of when it may be important to tune into your dreams:

- You rarely or "never" remember your dreams and you do.

- A deceased loved one appears in physical form or "in essence" For instance, it didn't look like your Grandmother, but you could sense her. Perhaps you were talking to a tree but you knew you were conversing with her.

- You act in a way that is out of alignment with your highest values and feel wracked with guilt. In recovery, relapse dreams are both common and, at times, helpful in maintaining one's commitment.

- The dream feels relevant to a decision you're making.

- The dream is powerfully tied to emotion

- The dream is repeated again and again and/or continues to develop over time.

Dreams have long been a part of spiritual practice and psychological exploration. Temples were once built for dreamers. Dreams reveal insights that can lead to emotional balance and physical wellbeing. Psychologists look to dreams to reveal parts of the psyche the conscious mind is unwilling to greet. The old testament speaks of Joseph interpreting dreams as an act of prophecy in prison.

I flew to Tacoma, Washington to visit Jay. At the time, our relationship remained relegated to the category of lovers without commitment or definitions. We ventured out of the city to visit Mt. Rainier. That day as we hiked, I put some space between myself and my companion. My head reached into my heart and exploded there. What the hell was I doing in Tacoma, visiting a man... okay, a boy really, I'd professed my love to in a van by the ocean in San Diego? Instead of expressing an equivocal sentiment, he'd booked a flight to Tacoma and MOVED THERE within the week!

Honestly, I knew why I was there. The day I had arrived in Tacoma, not hours after he'd scooped me from the airport, Jay received a phone call. The voice on the other line lovingly informed him that his Father had uttered his last battle cry against his terminal cancer. I'd arrived in time to hold him while he mourned his father's passing. It had been an honourable mission. Now it was time to pack my bags and make the journey back home to bury my love as well. At least, I thought it was time. I made a little pact with myself on Mount Rainier to walk away from Jay forever.

That night Jay dreamt his Father, in full health, strolled up to him. His Dad expressed his love and his apologies. Dream me sat at Jay's side. His father gazed at us both lovingly. He gave our relationship his blessing. Then Jay turned to dream me and told me he loved me, which is exactly what he told me the following morning. The spirit of Jay's father or perhaps Jay's subconscious recognized a few things that conscious Jay did not. For one, Love and Forgiveness matter. It matters when we receive it from others and it most certainly matters when we offer it to ourselves. We need not be stingy with either. Second, despite my previous resolve, my love and I were not done.

Without that profession of love, I'd have cut my losses and returned home to lick my wounds. My plane departed that evening and I had no plans of returning to chase down unrequited or unspoken love. Without that dream, he wouldn't have broken through his grief in time to profess his love. It would have been our end. His conscious mind wasn't ready. Don't get me wrong, there was an end to that relationship, or at least to the committed, romantic incarnation of it, (please see hella dramatic, beach side break-up) but there was A LOT of learning yet to take place. Thank Intuition for sending in the big guns of a nocturnal visitor. I will never forget the drama and the downpour of obsessive love that rained on me that morning.

Let us speak of outrageous things, like dreams.

THE WORK

Relay a meaningful, prominent, or repeating dream of your very own.

What emotions were tied to the dream?

How did you discern this dream to be meaningful?

Write your interpretation of this dream. If you haven't deciphered one, try spit balling! Make it up! Guess! Visit the dream as vividly as you can, then write out the first things that come to mind. Feel free to assign metaphorical meaning to the characters, places, objects, or animals encountered.

Relay a meaningful, prominent, or repeating dream of your very own.

What emotions were tied to the dream?

How did you discern this dream to be meaningful?

Write your interpretation of this dream. If you haven't deciphered one, try spit balling! Feel free to assign metaphorical meaning to the characters, places, objects, or animals encountered.

206

Relay a meaningful, prominent, or repeating dream of your very own.

What emotions were tied to the dream?

How did you discern this dream to be meaningful?

Write your interpretation of this dream. If you haven't deciphered one, try spit balling! Feel free to assign metaphorical meaning to the characters, places, objects, or animals encountered.

SECTION 9: PRESCRIPTION STRENGTH DETANGLER

"If we have no peace, it is because we have forgotten that we belong to each other."

- Mother Teresa

We flashed past it with brevity, but a HUGE concept looms inside the dream of Jay's Dad, namely forgiveness. Informing me when it's time to forgive is one of the key roles Intuition plays in my life.

It also frequently informs me when I'm ripe to take a big ole swig of humility to wash down that nasty taste of the pride I'm swallowing. It sends the desire and the willpower to dole out an admittance of my shortcomings and a plan to do better in the future. Leaving the timing up to Intuition is paramount. If we forgive too soon, surrendering our protective

209

rage, our kind boundaries, or the county lines we've crossed to get ourselves out of a shitty situation, forgiveness won't be safe. Forgiveness is a form of self-care not masochism. If you are being harmed by another person (not to be confused with harming yourself through other people or your own perspective), by all means, get pissed and angry. Communicate this anger, and definitely, *definitely* GET AWAY from that person!

At nineteen in Utah, while abandoning all aspects of faith, I became recklessly and addictively obsessed with my best friend, Mike. He didn't love me... I mean, he told me he loved me, but he lacked my fervor and meant it as friendship. We frequently fondled each other until we could bare it no longer. We fell deeper into intimacy. We'd race each other to oblivion with shots of vodka, and sometimes gin, and occasionally whiskey to assuage the guilt of our mutual Mormon upbringings. Then, we'd roll around in his twin bed which, much like Mike's heart, didn't have much room for me. It wasn't the right size or shape. It wasn't made to hold me. There were SO many mistakes, so many ruthless decisions, so much manipulation, game-playing, and jealousy, and plenty of lies of omission.

For my part, I blamed him for my addiction and inability to walk away. I played the victim like a prima donna begging for her first two-bit part, shamelessly, with gusto, and completely oblivious to my inconsistencies and imperfections. I performed for Mike as well. I wore sexy like a costume. When it started to slip or rip, I'd cling to it. I was desperate for sexy to save me from the sickness that sunk in during the wake of his purely physical love. I blamed this sickness on the booze and spent many hours crying on toilet seats, cradling my belly with my arms and rocking to the incessant internal screaming, "Why doesn't he love me?" Ugh. I do not miss those times.

To circle back, I left. I moved to Alaska. (See page one.) My addiction required detox! I also possessed a grand total of zero tools for coping with this type of fall-out. So, I packed up the blame and the shame and the victimhood. I scooped up the story of the weak, little girl who hid herself to please a person who yearned only for her body. I stored it all in a box. I put that box in a closet in the back of my chest and I hid it from myself.

Fast forward ten years. I find myself seated in the office of a fabulously effective psychologist. I hired her (okay, begged her) to help me weed through the cow caca I'd landed in when I was flung free of the Jay bull ride. Surprise! Surprise! Amidst the cattle crap, I located the box that held my manipulative first love.

This box housed moldy memories of swallowing "no" and caving to pressure. It held his inclination to try to share my body with people I didn't lust for or trust. It housed the sensation of being used. It held his silence, the way he hid and isolated and shut down when the sadness came, just like me. It lodged a vow I'd written to myself, like Scarlett O'Hara's haunting promise to "never go hungry again!" My haunted heart proclaimed, "I'll never be weak again!" I'll never dance provocatively because a man with empty hands and a sick soul wants to see something pretty and touch it and taste it and waste it. No dance, no costume, no woman can fill the void of an empty heart.

One night, I sat wrapped in a blanket under the full moon and whispered the worst memories of Mike and I's time together. I also cataloged the best memories and the ample lessons. I recalled the time I tried to cover my chest with my crossed arms and he gently took my wrists and asks me not to hide. "You're beautiful. Please don't cover it up." he entreated seriously. Then he kissed my forehead, my cheeks, and the line of my belly.

I can't count how many cackles we accumulated. Mike's dry wit and shocking behavior frequently dropped my jaw and tested the stamina of my cheeks to sustain the laughter. I also spoke aloud why it needed to end. I whispered to the night why I had to go. I reaffirmed to the moon that this man was never MY man, just a friend/foe who tasted and tainted me.

These spoken words rained down revelation. My empathy for this person swelled, yet despite my desire to forgive him, I still resented that relationship. It still itched and burned. The box was open, sorted, clean, yet still in my hands and in my heart.

Years prior to this moon magic and therapy session, Mike and I reconnected. He flew to my city, spent the day with me, bought me martinis, and apologized. He told me he hadn't recognized how special I was to him. I replied that I already knew, and he was already forgiven.

At the time, I thought I spoke the truth. He requested I come upstairs to avoid being seen in the bar late at night by his colleagues. In his hotel room, he nestled me into his chest and promptly fell asleep. Back in Utah, his current girlfriend slept presumably alone. I lay in the dark, feeling small and lost and tragic. How could I let him drape his arm over me? How could I be as weak and helpless as I'd been years before. It took all my strength to slide out from under his arm, collect my bag from the cool hotel room floor and drive Spartacus home. The next time I saw him he was cold and distant and drunk. Just like old times.

A few months after I told our story to the moon, I flew to Utah for a friend's wedding. I will always think of Mike in the Salt Lake City airport. I still scan for his face when the fast-paced stride of a pilot passes me. After arriving in Salt Lake City, his home and the site of his recent matrimony, I picked up my phone and sent off this text: "Congratulations on your marriage! If I see you down the line, I'd love to meet her."

This text carried multiple meanings. Firstly, it felt important to compassionately and genuinely wish him well. Secondly, I wanted to acknowledge and honour his marriage. I meant to imply that we'd only see each other again if his wife was present. This requirement seemed valid given our history. I truthfully didn't expect a response. Our past was bloated by his radio silence. I sent the words and the sentiment anyway.

The next morning, I awoke to a text message. It read: "Thanks, Anika. That means a lot. I hope you are well." I sat silently on the bed. Surprise and appreciation rippled through my body. In my heart, a door that had been cracked open and drafty for years, quietly, without fanfare, clicked shut. I scanned for the box that lived in my body labelled "Mike." I couldn't locate it. It'd disappeared. In its place sat empathy for all the insecurities that made Mike exactly the person he'd been back then and for the married man who existed today. Not love, empathy. I shed a few shocked tears at my newly found truth. This marked the moment I truly forgave Mike. I also believe it marked our final goodbye.

Resentments fester. They eat us from the inside. When we hold our anger longer than we need it, it stops being helpful and transfigures into a parasite. So be mad! Then, when you're ready, open up that box of resentment and rage you shoved into the cancerous closet that houses all the things you don't want anyone (including yourself) to see. Unpack that shit. This will not be easy. There's a reason you packed it up and hid it from yourself. It will burn and puss like an infected wound reopened and scrubbed with rough bristles. You'll feel like you're walking around with an itchy scab on your heart for a while. Then, when you least expect it, Intuition, in its wisdom and glory, will wave its wand of wonder and you'll note the wound is healed. You are whole. You were always whole, even when you were itchy.

Hark! The sound of the closet door creaking open...

THE WORK

Lay out a memorable or recent time you offered forgiveness.

Stipulate the process that allowed you to be able to forgive? Was it instantaneous and easy? (Sometimes, it is.) Did it require cataloging events and accepting your part? How did you cultivate empathy? Were you forced to set aside your need to be right in order to be compassionate?

Outline the timeline. Did forgiveness come in waves? How long did it take? What or who determined the timing?

How did it feel to forgive? Did it compromise your safety? Did a door click shut in your heart? Did you set down a metaphorical backpack? Are you relieved? Do you remain or did you become empowered? Has the situation lost its emotional charge? Have you shed a karmic debt or ended a karmic cycle (or old pattern of behavior)?

Lay out a memorable or recent time you offered forgiveness.

Stipulate the process that allowed you to be able to forgive? Was it instantaneous and easy? (Sometimes, it is.) Did it require cataloging events and accepting your part? How did you cultivate empathy? Were you forced to set aside your need to be right in order to be compassionate?

Outline the timeline. Did forgiveness come in waves? How long did it take? What or who determined the timing?

How did it feel to forgive?

Finally, how does this apply to Intuition? Looking at the above examples, did your Intuition nudge you in the direction of forgiveness? If so how? With regard to the timeline, would you have been ready to forgive earlier if you'd been asked? How did Intuition employ timing that supported your safety and readiness?

Now let's look at this from the reverse angle. If you're familiar with a twelve-step program, you probably know that part of the schtick is making amends. (Step nine, yo!) That means composing a thorough list of everything you've done to harm anyone in YOUR ENTIRE LIFE, then proceeding to contact and apologize to EVERY ONE OF THEM! On top of that, you ask them if there's anything you can do to set it right, and if it's feasible and they ask it, you do it. (That reminds me, I need to call my mother.) This is no joke. It's actually the most humbling endeavor I've ever pursued. It was also one of the most gut-wrenchingly beautiful. I'd compare it to going back through the web of connection that weaves love and belonging into our lives, (you know, in my opinion, the reason we're alive) and untangling any knotted, matted sections. It required accepting that once woven into one another's lives, like it or not, we cannot be unwoven. We have two choices: tend to the web or become tangled in it. We can pretend we are not intertwined, but this is denial. If we exist, then the web exists. We are only as well as the web.

I learned through step nine that forgiveness is a gift. It will not be delivered on demand. In order to be forgiven, every one of us fallible humans hangs dependent on another's mercy, or at the mercy of our own tender hearts. When someone refused to take my call, answer my email, or hear my belated apology, the task of mercy fell to me. I had to tell all the creatures in the cancerous closet that we'd done the best we could, that we would do better, and they didn't have to stay in hiding anymore. I cradled my darkest deeds when no one else would hold them. I told them there was still time. I even told them I loved them.

On the other hand, many individuals offered mercy without knowing they were performing a miracle. After months of not speaking, I proffered Lena a long-deserved apology. She'd been bludgeoned by my demonic detachment when I crossed the threshold into what I'm told is terrifyingly cold fury. Similar to the dementors of Harry Potter, I'd shifted into an icy, unseeing specter who seemed completely willing to erase her soul. Before I could complete my guilty admission, she reached across the table to bolster my strength by holding my hand.

Another compadre, Casey, took the opportunity of our tears and tea session to open up her own box of buried missteps. In other cases, clarity rained down on misunderstandings. Some people assured me they never thought of said missteps and begged me not berate myself. When I told my parents of my alcoholism and professed my immense sorrow that I'd wounded them with my isolation, my Dad tripped in his attempt to console me. He actually tripped. (We were walking.) Words cannot do justice to the miracle of mercy.

Behold, the magic of mercy!

THE WORK

Cite an instance in which you felt inspired to apologize, make amends, or ask for forgiveness.

How did Intuition encourage you to untie this knot in your web of intimacy and support? Did the apology fly out unexpectedly? Were you overcome with desire? Did guilt slowly gnaw at your gut? Did you delay or procrastinate? Did the urge strike randomly on some idle Tuesday? Did someone else start the ball rolling?

How did it feel? How does it feel now?

Lay out the outcome? How were you received? Were you forgiven? How have you altered your behavior or mindset? What did you learn?

Cite an instance in which you felt inspired to apologize, make amends, or ask for forgiveness.

Include the aspect of timing. Did you delay or apologize in an instant? Did someone else start the ball rolling?

How did it feel? How does it feel now?

Lay out the outcome? How were you received? Were you forgiven? How has your behavior changed? What did you learn?

Cite an instance in which you felt inspired to apologize, make amends, or ask for forgiveness.

Include the aspect of timing. Did you delay or apologize in an instant? Did someone else start the ball rolling?

How did it feel?

Lay out the outcome? How were you received? Were you forgiven? How has this shaped your future behavior? What did you learn?

Is there anyone's name on a box in "the cancerous closet" that you'd like to open up and re-examine with or without professional help?

Disclaimer:

In instances of emotional or physical abuse, I highly recommend professional assistance. (Shoot. I'd recommend it to anyone who can afford it.) Even if professional help is a financial strain, for those who have experienced significant trauma, it's highly probable that guidance is necessary. There may be more financial options or resources available than you realize.

As a rule of thumb, try to stay in your body, aware of your seat, your skin, and your sensations in real time as you visit old memories. To put it another way, if you visit a memory so thoroughly that you forget that you are here and safe, please stop and seek consult. If you visit a memory and feel nothing at all, that is to say, feel numb and disconnected from your body, again, you are encouraged to seek professional guidance.

Should you feel resistance, annoyance, readiness, determination, frustration, love, or even fear, then buckle up, buckaroo! We're right on track! Call upon your courage and support if you need it! Let's open some boxes!

Is there anyone in your life who you are ready to forgive? What about institutions? (Both "Men" and "Mormonism" made it on my list.) List in a separate column any person or group you hope to forgive, but don't quite feel ready. It's okay to not be ready. Record your willingness.

Is it possible and beneficial to contact this person? Would a symbolic or simple gesture serve both parties?

If so, brainstorm ideas. Would you like to wish this person well in some way? Perhaps a letter, a text message, a phone call and/or an admission of your own missteps would tend to the current tangles in your web.(No harming! Kindness before confessions, please!) What are your motivations? Do you have expectations? Can you set them aside?

If no, what solo activities could solidify this ending? (Burning letters and crying under the moon are personal favorites.) You could also carry a rock with you for a few days, weeks, or months and drop it when you feel ready to forgive. You might tie a string around your wrist to be cut away in symbolic liberation. You could visualize this person, then tell them you love and forgive them. You could donate to a charity they support or play monopoly by their wrong rules. You might write a song, poem, or limerick to commemorate what you learned from one another. You could scream at the top of your lungs until you run out of breath and rage. Detail your favorite ideas below. Then circle a favorite or two. Then, try it! See what happens.

What happened?!?

Are you ready to forgive yourself for your human frailty? Are you ready to forgive yourself for something specific? Have you done everything in your power to make it right? Can you let it go now? Please speak to yourself mercifully as you outline your missed marks and breakdowns.

Homework: Offer a genuine apology without expectation or blame. When you can, when you're ready, when it's available and not a second before, forgive someone. Forgive yourself. Practice mercy.

SECTION 10:
"ACTION" FIGURES AND ROLE MODELS

"But a role model in the flesh provides more than inspiration; his or her very existence is confirmation of possibilities one may have every reason to doubt, saying, yes, someone like me can do this."

-Sonia Sotomayor

Like any good twenty-one-year-old on an adventure, the boytoy I selected to be my playmate for my first summer in Alaska sported a tongue ring, a Jack Kerouac tattoo, the morality of a thief, the attention span of a stoner, and the best intentions. Eddie's personality pops with charisma. For the majority of the time I've known him he's been paid to talk. He's worked as a professional tour guide, storyteller, and public speaker, but in the summer of our fleeting romance, he played the role of charming, quick-witted, and debaucherous bartender.

Eddie hails from Niagara Falls, New York. The neighboring town of Buffalo spawned the music icon, Ani Difranco. In a very correct assessment of my tastes, he introduced me to her brilliant personality, raw lyrics, and badass talent. In his apartment that smelled of homemade hummus and Barefoot Wine, he pulled up a video online of a small woman with wild hair sitting on a stool with her guitar. When she sang the words, "Tell you the truth I prefer the worst of you, too bad you had to have a better half. She's not really my type, but I think you two are forever. I hate to say it, but you're perfect together, so fuck you." I tripped over my illusions of isolation and fell madly for the sounds and words that caused me to feel alive and less alone in my feverish and frustrating humanity. Thus, began a love affair that continues to date.

It's my guess that Intuition delivers the people who can inspire us. Sometimes these people are real, live, and tangible. They perform ferocious acts of bravery without too many people paying attention. It could be your twin, your mother, or the woman down the street who sings when she hangs her clothes out on the line. She or He may be a superhero of the floating icon variety. The ones who put their bleeding hearts and callused hands into projects. They may even give their whole lives to a cause or passion. Maybe they are exceptional at just one thing, and they remind you that you too can be completely screwed up in every aspect of your life and still be bloody brilliant at something.

I believe that Intuition leads us to hope, action, generosity, forgiveness, love, and creation. If there are people on this planet that connect you to these things, you're encouraged to engage with inspiration through their presence. Stimulate your imagination by experiencing what they do. Sing along to their greatest hits. Initiate an appreciative phone conversation with your warrior of wisdom and whimsy. These are just a few ways to toss lighter fluid (in Montana we call it boy scout juice) on the fire of your blazing Intuition.

"The only people for me are the mad ones, the ones who are mad to live, mad to talk, mad to be saved, desirous of everything at the same time, the ones who never yawn or say a commonplace thing, but burn, burn, burn like fabulous yellow roman candles exploding like spiders across the stars and in the middle you see the blue centerlight pop and everybody goes "Awww!"

-Jack Kerouac in On The Road

Let's find out who sports your favorite brand of madness.

THE WORK

List a few people, icons, or close proximity comrades who inspire you, exhibit traits or leave a legacy you admire, exemplify mastery of a craft, or radiate life and/or love.

Pick one of the above listed individuals and describe why you admire them. What about their being inspires you?

How do you feel when you are in contact with either this individual or what they offer to the world?

Consolidate into one or two sentences what this person or their work has shown you. Write the sentence or sentences below.

Pick a new choice from the above listed individuals and describe why you admire them. What about their being inspires you?

How do you feel when you are in contact with either this individual or what they offer into the world?

Consolidate into one or two sentences what this person or their work has shown you. Write the sentence or sentences below.

Pick another of the above listed individuals and describe why you admire them. What about their being inspires you?

How do you feel when you are in contact with either this individual or what they offer into the world?

Consolidate into one or two sentences what this person or their work has shown you. Write the sentence or sentences below.

Yet again, pick one of the above listed individuals and describe why you admire them. What about their being inspires you?

How do you feel when you are in contact with either this individual or what they offer into the world?

Consolidate into one or two sentences what this person or their work has shown you. Write the sentence or sentences below.

How are you making contact with each of your above listed inspirations? Does it appear that a practice of deliberately cultivating a closer proximity to these individuals or their work would be in your best interest? List why or why not for each:

Write yourself an inspiration to do list. How would you like to make contact with your Intuition through your role models? Would you like to schedule time with a mentor, call your mother, listen to recitations from your favorite poets? I, myself, am putting on an Ani Difranco album right now!

As you follow through with your "to-do list", fresh intuitive insights may reveal themselves to you. Perhaps this comes through feelings of wellbeing or even direct messages, feel free to list your revelations below:

SECTION 11:
POWERFUL MYTHS AND FAMILIAR FORCES

"All the gods, all the heavens, all the hells, are within you."

— Joseph Campbell

In the previous section we discussed "Live Action," or, to use a different word, "living" role models. Yet to connect to your own intuitive nature, the inspiration doesn't necessarily need to come from something or someone living or even real. One might, and people frequently do, extract immense amounts of wisdom and peace from iconic stories or myths. It may be less common but still fairly frequent that people sense the realm of spirit or communicate with the souls of passed loved ones. We've all at least spoken to someone who declares themselves connected to or protected by a friend, pet, parent, or grandparent who by all observable evidence has left the planet. Others fasten faith to familiar forces watching over them that may be unnamed or not necessarily human.

I'm less concerned with the "reality" of these allegations and more enthralled with the affect these said beliefs have on the person in question. Does this person experience a life ripe with joy for their picking? Does this connection with ancestry keep them looking for beauty and meaning? Does the thought of aliens watching over you and guarding your back with lasers help you sleep at night? We can debate aliens until the cows come home, but I think we can all get behind the concept of sleep! Do you need to "know" in order to extract the perks?

In regard to story, more often than not, we are aware when we are reading or listening to a piece of fiction. For instance, I have devoted a large lump of time to reading the thirteen book fantasy series The Wheel of Time by Robert Jordan. (Nerd alert!) The author wove a plot so exceedingly lengthy and intricate that he ACTUALLY DIED before he could finish the series. Prior to his death, he and his wife commissioned Brandon Sanderson to complete the last three novels. These books, while fables, taught me to look for the beauty and humor hidden in forsaken circumstances. It depicted leaders forged by strength, integrity, and intelligence. It portrayed powerful women. The story cursed and lauded destiny and relished in dignity. A theme sleeps in the bed of any great story. Without that body, it's just a bit of fluff without a purpose.

With this in mind, let's begin:

THE WORK

What is your favorite story or myth?

What is the theme of this story?

Who is the hero or heroine? What draws you to this character?

How does this story relate to your UNIQUE Intuition? Speculate on the story's allure. If this story had a message for you specifically, what would the message be?

Describe a new story or myth that speaks to you:

What is the theme of this story?

Who is the hero or heroine? What draws you to this character?

How does this story relate to your UNIQUE Intuition? Speculate on the story's allure. If this story had a message for you specifically, what would the message be?

Pick another story or fable or myth?

What is the theme of this story?

Who is the hero or heroine? What draws you to this character?

How does this story relate to your UNIQUE Intuition? Speculate on the story's allure. If this story had a message for you specifically, what would the message be?

Okay let's get weird. Talk to me of spirits.

Have you interacted or thought you interacted with a spirit that was not living in this realm? This could include, but need not be limited to, spirits who have passed, spirits yet to be born, dead loved ones, aliens, or forces. If so, please describe. If not, move on to the next exercise or have your "kooky friend" fill out this section.

List the aspects of the experience that led you to believe you were being contacted.

Do you believe this force (or forces) had your best interest or the best interest of another human at heart? Did you perceive this force to be neutral or malicious? Why or why not?

What did you learn or gather from this experience?

Please describe or have your kooky friend describe another interaction with a force outside the human realm:

List the aspects of the experience that led you to believe you were being contacted.

Do you believe this force had your best interest or the best interest of another human at heart? Did you perceive this force to be neutral or malicious? Why or why not?

What did you learn or gather from this experience?

Please describe or have your kooky friend describe another interaction with a force outside the human realm:

List the aspects of the experience that led you to believe you were being contacted.

Do you believe this force had your best interest or the best interest of another human at heart? Did you perceive this force to be neutral of malicious? Why or why not?

What did you learn or gather from this experience?

Please describe or have your kooky friend describe another interaction with a force outside the human realm:

List the aspects of the experience that led you to believe you were being contacted.

Do you believe this force had your best interest or the best interest of another human at heart? Did you perceive this force to be neutral or malicious? Why or why not?

What did you learn or gather from this experience?

SECTION 12: HIT OR MISS

"It is common sense to take a method and try it. If it fails, admit it frankly and try another. But above all, try something."

— Franklin D. Roosevelt

We've explored a variety of ways to access and explore Intuition. Now comes the component I personally have never excelled at consistently implementing... namely practice. The following pages are worksheets for identifying and working with intuitive "hits" you receive or think you may have received. Your quest is to learn to recognize wisdom and respond from that recognition. Rarely do we instantly ascertain our accuracy through evidence. In some cases, we never receive confirmation that our "hunch" was credible. In the following exercise, log the potential intuitive "hit" when it wallops you in the face or whispers coyly. Then, leave the assessment portion for a later date once events and time have splashed you with truth serum and gifted you hindsight. Like all the other practices, there's just as much to be gleaned from intuitive misses as from intuitive hits, so please invite all the fuck-ups to the party. We love fuck-ups. (Okay. I'm LEARNING to love fuck-ups.) Plus, this exercise will go on repeating, so you'll have plenty of chances to revel in the glory of hitting the bullseye.

Progress, not perfection they say.

THE WORK

Inciting Incident: Describe the impulse, feeling, thought, idea, omen, image, dream, coincidence, visualization, chance encounter, or loss of control you believe to be the voice of Intuition. Get specific. Were any of the five senses involved? Where were you? Who were you with? What emotions accompanied this experience?

Registration and Interpretation: How did you interpret this experience? Why did you find it relevant? What was the timeline of your interpretation? Did you register this as Intuition right away or did it sink in later? Did you think, "I knew it!" after your insight came to fruition? Did you sense these events or feelings to be important without necessarily being able to decipher why?

269

State of Mind and Body: Immediately preceding this occurrence what was your state of mind? What (if anything) were you thinking? What was your physical location? What was your physical state? (well rested? hungry? relaxed?) What was your emotional and mental state? (Agitated? Excited? Ruminating? Scared? Inquisitive?) Had you recently set an intention? Were you desperate? Did you feel open?

Reaction/Action: Did you immediately or instinctively respond to these stimuli? Did you consciously choose an action? Why or why not? Did you put this experience in words through a journal? Did you verbally share it with a confidante? If the insight was for someone else, did you relay it to them? Why did you decide this was appropriate? Was this share welcome? How did this person react?

When all is revealed, (or at least enough is revealed to assess accuracy), record the results.

Outcome: What happened? How did this play out in the short term? If the insight is in reference to a more distant future, feel free to leave this section blank until the results become clearer.

Correlation: What did this teach you about your relationship with Intuition? What did you learn about your personal intuitive language? What notes would you give yourself for the future?

Application: Extract the juice of the insight! Aside from learning about your intuitive language, what did you learn about you or life itself from this experience? In one or two sentences, outline the theme of this experience. Then list three takeaways. If the takeaways aren't clear, make a few educated guesses or let the uncertainty brew for a while. Tasting the soup along the way is great, but feel free to let it simmer! Fabulous soup and delicious insights are worth the wait!

Conscious Connection: This time instead of waiting for Intuition to strike like lightning and singe you down to your socks, imagine it already lives and whispers from inside of you. Perhaps, Intuition patiently waits for you to be ready to listen. Lean into the current of your intuitive stream. Using what you've observed in previous pages, feel into the place in your body where you believe (or make-believe, if you rather) Intuition dwells. Give this place or feeling or current a voice. What does it say? Write the words here.

Inciting Incident: Describe the impulse, feeling, thought, idea, omen, image, dream, coincidence, visualization, chance encounter, or loss of control you believe to be the voice of Intuition. Get specific. Were any of the five senses involved? Where were you? Who were you with? What emotions accompanied this experience?

Registration and Interpretation: How did you interpret this experience? Why did you find it relevant? What was the timeline of your interpretation? Did you register this as Intuition right away or did it sink in later? Did you think, "I knew it!" after your insight came to fruition? Did you sense these events or feelings to be important without necessarily being able to decipher why?

State of Mind and Body: Immediately preceding this occurrence what was your state of mind? What (if anything) were you thinking about? What was your physical location? What was your physical state? What was your emotional and mental state? Had you recently set an intention? Were you desperate? Did you feel open?

Reaction/Action: Did you immediately or instinctively respond to this stimulus? Did you consciously choose to act on this stimulus? Why or why not? In what way did you share or record this experience?

Record the results.

Outcome: What happened? How did this play out in the short term? If the insight is in reference to a more distant future, leave this section blank until the results become clearer.

Correlation: What did this teach you about your relationship with Intuition? What did you learn about your personal intuitive language? What notes would you give yourself for the future?

Application: Extract the juice of the insight! Aside from learning about your intuitive language, what did you learn about yourself or about life itself? In one or two sentences, outline the theme of this experience. Then list three takeaways. If the takeaways aren't clear, make a few educated guesses or let the uncertainty brew for a while.

Conscious Connection: Imagine Intuition lives and whispers from inside of you. Lean into the current of your intuitive stream. Using what you've observed in previous pages, feel into the place in your body where you believe (or make-believe, if you rather) Intuition dwells. Give this place or feeling or current a voice. What does it say? Write the words here.

Inciting Incident: Describe the impulse, feeling, thought, idea, omen, image, dream, coincidence, visualization, chance encounter, or loss of control you believe to be the voice of Intuition. Get specific. Were any of the five senses involved? Where were you? Who were you with? What emotions accompanied this experience?

Registration and Interpretation: How did you interpret this experience? Why did you find it relevant? What was the timeline of your interpretation? Did you register this as Intuition right away or did it sink in later? Did you think, "I knew it!" after your insight came to fruition? Did you sense these events or feelings to be important without necessarily being able to decipher why?

State of Mind and Body: Immediately preceding this occurrence what was your state of mind? What (if anything) were you thinking about? What was your physical location? What was your physical state? What was your emotional and mental state? Had you recently set an intention? Were you desperate? Did you feel open?

Reaction/Action: Did you immediately or instinctively respond to this stimulus? Did you consciously choose to act on this stimulus? Why or why not? In what way did you share or record this experience?

Record the results.

Outcome: What happened? How did this play out in the short term? If the insight is in reference to a more distant future, leave this section blank until the results become clearer.

Correlation: What did this teach you about your relationship with Intuition? What did you learn about your personal intuitive language? What notes would you give yourself for the future?

Application: Extract the juice of the insight! Aside from learning about your intuitive language, what did you learn about yourself or about life itself? In one or two sentences, outline the theme of this experience. Then list three takeaways. If the takeaways aren't clear, make a few educated guesses or let the uncertainty brew for a while.

Conscious Connection: Imagine Intuition lives and whispers from inside of you. Lean into the current of your intuitive stream. Using what you've observed in previous pages, feel into the place in your body where you believe (or make-believe, if you rather) Intuition dwells. Give this place or feeling or current a voice. What does it say? Write the words here.

Inciting Incident: Describe the impulse, feeling, thought, idea, omen, image, dream, coincidence, visualization, chance encounter, or loss of control you believe to be the voice of Intuition. Get specific. Were any of the five senses involved? Where were you? Who were you with? What emotions accompanied this experience?

Registration and Interpretation: How did you interpret this experience? Why did you find it relevant? What was the timeline of your interpretation? Did you register this as Intuition right away or did it sink in later? Did you think, "I knew it!" after your insight came to fruition? Did you sense these events or feelings to be important without necessarily being able to decipher why?

State of Mind and Body: Immediately preceding this occurrence what was your state of mind? What (if anything) were you thinking about? What was your physical location? What was your physical state? What was your emotional and mental state? Had you recently set an intention? Were you desperate? Did you feel open?

Reaction/Action: Did you immediately or instinctively respond to this stimulus? Did you consciously choose to act on this stimulus? Why or why not? In what way did you share or record this experience?

Record the results.

Outcome: What happened? How did this play out in the short term? If the insight is in reference to a more distant future, leave this section blank until the results become clearer.

Correlation: What did this teach you about your relationship with Intuition? What did you learn about your personal intuitive language? What notes would you give yourself for the future?

Application: Extract the juice of the insight! Aside from learning about your intuitive language, what did you learn about yourself or about life itself? In one or two sentences, outline the theme of this experience. Then list three takeaways. If the takeaways aren't clear, make a few educated guesses or let the uncertainty brew for a while.

Conscious Connection: Imagine Intuition lives and whispers from inside of you. Lean into the current of your intuitive stream. Using what you've observed in previous pages, feel into the place in your body where you believe (or make-believe, if you rather) Intuition dwells. Give this place or feeling or current a voice. What does it say? Write the words here.

Inciting Incident: Describe the impulse, feeling, thought, idea, omen, image, dream, coincidence, visualization, chance encounter, or loss of control you believe to be the voice of Intuition. Get specific. Were any of the five senses involved? Where were you? Who were you with? What emotions accompanied this experience?

Registration and Interpretation: How did you interpret this experience? Why did you find it relevant? What was the timeline of your interpretation? Did you register this as Intuition right away or did it sink in later? Did you think, "I knew it!" after your insight came to fruition? Did you sense these events or feelings to be important without necessarily being able to decipher why?

State of Mind and Body: Immediately preceding this occurrence what was your state of mind? What (if anything) were you thinking about? What was your physical location? What was your physical state? What was your emotional and mental state? Had you recently set an intention? Were you desperate? Did you feel open?

Reaction/Action: Did you immediately or instinctively respond to this stimulus? Did you consciously choose to act on this stimulus? Why or why not? In what way did you share or record this experience?

Record the results.

Outcome: What happened? How did this play out in the short term? If the insight is in reference to a more distant future, leave this section blank until the results become clearer.

Correlation: What did this teach you about your relationship with Intuition? What did you learn about your personal intuitive language? What notes would you give yourself for the future?

Application: Extract the juice of the insight! Aside from learning about your intuitive language, what did you learn about yourself or about life itself? In one or two sentences, outline the theme of this experience. Then list three takeaways. If the takeaways aren't clear, make a few educated guesses or let the uncertainty brew for a while.

Conscious Connection: Imagine Intuition lives and whispers from inside of you. Lean into the current of your intuitive stream. Using what you've observed in previous pages, feel into the place in your body where you believe (or make-believe, if you rather) Intuition dwells. Give this place or feeling or current a voice. What does it say? Write the words here.

Inciting Incident: Describe the impulse, feeling, thought, idea, omen, image, dream, coincidence, visualization, chance encounter, or loss of control you believe to be the voice of Intuition. Get specific. Were any of the five senses involved? Where were you? Who were you with? What emotions accompanied this experience?

Registration and Interpretation: How did you interpret this experience? Why did you find it relevant? What was the timeline of your interpretation? Did you register this as Intuition right away or did it sink in later? Did you think, "I knew it!" after your insight came to fruition? Did you sense these events or feelings to be important without necessarily being able to decipher why?

State of Mind and Body: Immediately preceding this occurrence what was your state of mind? What (if anything) were you thinking about? What was your physical location? What was your physical state? What was your emotional and mental state? Had you recently set an intention? Were you desperate? Did you feel open?

Reaction/Action: Did you immediately or instinctively respond to this stimulus? Did you consciously choose to act on this stimulus? Why or why not? In what way did you share or record this experience?

Record the results.

Outcome: What happened? How did this play out in the short term? If the insight is in reference to a more distant future, leave this section blank until the results become clearer.

Correlation: What did this teach you about your relationship with Intuition? What did you learn about your personal intuitive language? What notes would you give yourself for the future?

Application: Extract the juice of the insight! Aside from learning about your intuitive language, what did you learn about yourself or about life itself? In one or two sentences, outline the theme of this experience. Then, list three takeaways. If the takeaways aren't clear, make a few educated guesses or let the uncertainty brew for a while.

Conscious Connection: Imagine Intuition lives and whispers from inside of you. Lean into the current of your intuitive stream. Using what you've observed in previous pages, feel into the place in your body where you believe (or make-believe, if you rather) Intuition dwells. Give this place or feeling or current a voice. What does it say? Write the words here.

Inciting Incident: Describe the impulse, feeling, thought, idea, omen, image, dream, coincidence, visualization, chance encounter, or loss of control you believe to be the voice of Intuition. Get specific. Were any of the five senses involved? Where were you? Who were you with? What emotions accompanied this experience?

Registration and Interpretation: How did you interpret this experience? Why did you find it relevant? What was the timeline of your interpretation? Did you register this as Intuition right away or did it sink in later? Did you think, "I knew it!" after your insight came to fruition? Did you sense these events or feelings to be important without necessarily being able to decipher why?

State of Mind and Body: Immediately preceding this occurrence what was your state of mind? What (if anything) were you thinking about? What was your physical location? What was your physical state? What was your emotional and mental state? Had you recently set an intention? Were you desperate? Did you feel open?

Reaction/Action: Did you immediately or instinctively respond to this stimulus? Did you consciously choose to act on this stimulus? Why or why not? In what way did you share or record this experience?

Record the results

Outcome: What happened? How did this play out in the short term? If the insight is in reference to a more distant future, leave this section blank until the results become clearer.

Correlation: What did this teach you about your relationship with Intuition? What did you learn about your personal intuitive language? What notes would you give yourself for the future?

Application: Extract the juice of the insight! Aside from learning about your intuitive language, what did you learn about yourself or about life itself? In one or two sentences, outline the theme of this experience. Then list three takeaways. If the takeaways aren't clear, make a few educated guesses or let the uncertainty brew for a while.

Conscious Connection: Imagine Intuition lives and whispers from inside of you. Lean into the current of your intuitive stream. Using what you've observed in previous pages, feel into the place in your body where you believe (or make-believe, if you rather) Intuition dwells. Give this place or feeling or current a voice. What does it say? Write the words here.

Inciting Incident: Describe the impulse, feeling, thought, idea, omen, image, dream, coincidence, visualization, chance encounter, or loss of control you believe to be the voice of Intuition. Get specific. Were any of the five senses involved? Where were you? Who were you with? What emotions accompanied this experience?

Registration and Interpretation: How did you interpret this experience? Why did you find it relevant? What was the timeline of your interpretation? Did you register this as Intuition right away or did it sink in later? Did you think, "I knew it!" after your insight came to fruition? Did you sense these events or feelings to be important without necessarily being able to decipher why?

State of Mind and Body: Immediately preceding this occurrence what was your state of mind? What (if anything) were you thinking about? What was your physical location? What was your physical state? What was your emotional and mental state? Had you recently set an intention? Were you desperate? Did you feel open?

Reaction/Action: Did you immediately or instinctively respond to this stimulus? Did you consciously choose to act on this stimulus? Why or why not? In what way did you share or record this experience?

Record the results.

Outcome: What happened? How did this play out in the short term? If the insight is in reference to a more distant future, leave this section blank until the results become clearer.

Correlation: What did this teach you about your relationship with Intuition? What did you learn about your personal intuitive language? What notes would you give yourself for the future?

Application: Extract the juice of the insight! Aside from learning about your intuitive language, what did you learn about yourself or about life itself? In one or two sentences, outline the theme of this experience. Then list three takeaways. If the takeaways aren't clear, make a few educated guesses or let the uncertainty brew for a while.

Conscious Connection: Imagine Intuition lives and whispers from inside of you. Lean into the current of your intuitive stream. Using what you've observed in previous pages, feel into the place in your body where you believe (or make-believe, if you rather) Intuition dwells. Give this place or feeling or current a voice. What does it say? Write the words here.

Inciting Incident: Describe the impulse, feeling, thought, idea, omen, image, dream, coincidence, visualization, chance encounter, or loss of control you believe to be the voice of Intuition. Get specific. Were any of the five senses involved? Where were you? Who were you with? What emotions accompanied this experience?

Registration and Interpretation: How did you interpret this experience? Why did you find it relevant? What was the timeline of your interpretation? Did you register this as Intuition right away or did it sink in later? Did you think, "I knew it!" after your insight came to fruition? Did you sense these events or feelings to be important without necessarily being able to decipher why?

State of Mind and Body: Immediately preceding this occurrence what was your state of mind? What (if anything) were you thinking about? What was your physical location? What was your physical state? What was your emotional and mental state? Had you recently set an intention? Were you desperate? Did you feel open?

Reaction/Action: Did you immediately or instinctively respond to this stimulus? Did you consciously choose to act on this stimulus? Why or why not? In what way did you share or record this experience?

Record the results.

Outcome: What happened? How did this play out in the short term? If the insight is in reference to a more distant future, leave this section blank until the results become clearer.

Correlation: What did this teach you about your relationship with Intuition? What did you learn about your personal intuitive language? What notes would you give yourself for the future?

Application: Extract the juice of the insight! Aside from learning about your intuitive language, what did you learn about yourself or about life itself? In one or two sentences, outline the theme of this experience. Then list three takeaways. If the takeaways aren't clear, make a few educated guesses or let the uncertainty brew for a while.

Conscious Connection: Imagine Intuition lives and whispers from inside of you. Lean into the current of your intuitive stream. Using what you've observed in previous pages, feel into the place in your body where you believe (or make-believe, if you rather) Intuition dwells. Give this place or feeling or current a voice. What does it say? Write the words here.

Inciting Incident: Describe the impulse, feeling, thought, idea, omen, image, dream, coincidence, visualization, chance encounter, or loss of control you believe to be the voice of Intuition. Get specific. Were any of the five senses involved? Where were you? Who were you with? What emotions accompanied this experience?

Registration and Interpretation: How did you interpret this experience? Why did you find it relevant? What was the timeline of your interpretation? Did you register this as Intuition right away or did it sink in later? Did you think, "I knew it!" after your insight came to fruition? Did you sense these events or feelings to be important without necessarily being able to decipher why?

State of Mind and Body: Immediately preceding this occurrence what was your state of mind? What (if anything) were you thinking about? What was your physical location? What was your physical state? What was your emotional and mental state? Had you recently set an intention? Were you desperate? Did you feel open?

Reaction/Action: Did you immediately or instinctively respond to this stimulus? Did you consciously choose to act on this stimulus? Why or why not? In what way did you share or record this experience?

Record the results.

Outcome: What happened? How did this play out in the short term? If the insight is in reference to a more distant future, leave this section blank until the results become clearer.

Correlation: What did this teach you about your relationship with Intuition? What did you learn about your personal intuitive language? What notes would you give yourself for the future?

Application: Extract the juice of the insight! Aside from learning about your intuitive language, what did you learn about yourself or about life itself? In one or two sentences, outline the theme of this experience. Then list three takeaways. If the takeaways aren't clear, make a few educated guesses or let the uncertainty brew for a while.

Conscious Connection: Imagine Intuition lives and whispers from inside of you. Lean into the current of your intuitive stream. Using what you've observed in previous pages, feel into the place in your body where you believe (or make-believe, if you rather) Intuition dwells. Give this place or feeling or current a voice. What does it say? Write the words here.

Inciting Incident: Describe the impulse, feeling, thought, idea, omen, image, dream, coincidence, visualization, chance encounter, or loss of control you believe to be the voice of Intuition. Get specific. Were any of the five senses involved? Where were you? Who were you with? What emotions accompanied this experience?

Registration and Interpretation: How did you interpret this experience? Why did you find it relevant? What was the timeline of your interpretation? Did you register this as Intuition right away or did it sink in later? Did you think, "I knew it!" after your insight came to fruition? Did you sense these events or feelings to be important without necessarily being able to decipher why?

State of Mind and Body: Immediately preceding this occurrence what was your state of mind? What (if anything) were you thinking about? What was your physical location? What was your physical state? What was your emotional and mental state? Had you recently set an intention? Were you desperate? Did you feel open?

Reaction/Action: Did you immediately or instinctively respond to this stimulus? Did you consciously choose to act on this stimulus? Why or why not? In what way did you share or record this experience?

Record the results

Outcome: What happened? How did this play out in the short term? If the insight is in reference to a more distant future, leave this section blank until the results become clearer.

Correlation: What did this teach you about your relationship with Intuition? What did you learn about your personal intuitive language? What notes would you give yourself for the future?

Application: Extract the juice of the insight! Aside from learning about your intuitive language, what did you learn about yourself or about life itself? In one or two sentences, outline the theme of this experience. Then list three takeaways. If the takeaways aren't clear, make a few educated guesses or let the uncertainty brew for a while.

Conscious Connection: Imagine Intuition lives and whispers from inside of you. Lean into the current of your intuitive stream. Using what you've observed in previous pages, feel into the place in your body where you believe (or make-believe, if you rather) Intuition dwells. Give this place or feeling or current a voice. What does it say? Write the words here.

Inciting Incident: Describe the impulse, feeling, thought, idea, omen, image, dream, coincidence, visualization, chance encounter, or loss of control you believe to be the voice of Intuition. Get specific. Were any of the five senses involved? Where were you? Who were you with? What emotions accompanied this experience?

Registration and Interpretation: How did you interpret this experience? Why did you find it relevant? What was the timeline of your interpretation? Did you register this as Intuition right away or did it sink in later? Did you think, "I knew it!" after your insight came to fruition? Did you sense these events or feelings to be important without necessarily being able to decipher why?

State of Mind and Body: Immediately preceding this occurrence what was your state of mind? What (if anything) were you thinking about? What was your physical location? What was your physical state? What was your emotional and mental state? Had you recently set an intention? Were you desperate? Did you feel open?

Reaction/Action: Did you immediately or instinctively respond to this stimulus? Did you consciously choose to act on this stimulus? Why or why not? In what way did you share or record this experience?

Record the results.

Outcome: What happened? How did this play out in the short term? If the insight is in reference to a more distant future, leave this section blank until the results become clearer.

Correlation: What did this teach you about your relationship with Intuition? What did you learn about your personal intuitive language? What notes would you give yourself for the future?

Application: Extract the juice of the insight! Aside from learning about your intuitive language, what did you learn about yourself or about life itself? In one or two sentences, outline the theme of this experience. Then list three takeaways. If the takeaways aren't clear, make a few educated guesses or let the uncertainty brew for a while.

Conscious Connection: Imagine Intuition lives and whispers from inside of you. Lean into the current of your intuitive stream. Using what you've observed in previous pages, feel into the place in your body where you believe (or make-believe, if you rather) Intuition dwells. Give this place or feeling or current a voice. What does it say? Write the words here.

Inciting Incident: Describe the impulse, feeling, thought, idea, omen, image, dream, coincidence, visualization, chance encounter, or loss of control you believe to be the voice of Intuition. Get specific. Were any of the five senses involved? Where were you? Who were you with? What emotions accompanied this experience?

Registration and Interpretation: How did you interpret this experience? Why did you find it relevant? What was the timeline of your interpretation? Did you register this as Intuition right away or did it sink in later? Did you think, "I knew it!" after your insight came to fruition? Did you sense these events or feelings to be important without necessarily being able to decipher why?

State of Mind and Body: Immediately preceding this occurrence what was your state of mind? What (if anything) were you thinking about? What was your physical location? What was your physical state? What was your emotional and mental state? Had you recently set an intention? Were you desperate? Did you feel open?

Reaction/Action: Did you immediately or instinctively respond to this stimulus? Did you consciously choose to act on this stimulus? Why or why not? In what way did you share or record this experience?

Record the results.

Outcome: What happened? How did this play out in the short term? If the insight is in reference to a more distant future, leave this section blank until the results become clearer.

Correlation: What did this teach you about your relationship with Intuition? What did you learn about your personal intuitive language? What notes would you give yourself for the future?

Application: Extract the juice of the insight! Aside from learning about your intuitive language, what did you learn about yourself or about life itself? In one or two sentences, outline the theme of this experience. Then list three takeaways. If the takeaways aren't clear, make a few educated guesses or let the uncertainty brew for a while.

Conscious Connection: Imagine Intuition lives and whispers from inside of you. Lean into the current of your intuitive stream. Using what you've observed in previous pages, feel into the place in your body where you believe (or make-believe, if you rather) Intuition dwells. Give this place or feeling or current a voice. What does it say? Write the words here.

SECTION 13:
ARE WE THERE YET?

"Listen to the wind, it talks. Listen to the silence, it speaks. Listen to your heart, it knows." Native American Proverb

Yowzers and congratulations! You've breezed or bumbled your way through increasing your fluency in your own intuitive language. I, myself, am a bumbler... (not the dating app) This is, of course, just the beginning, or the middle. (I mean, which life are you on?) Regardless of where you're currently camped on this backpacking trip of intuitive discovery, there's always room to hone your skills, sharpen your tools, and enrich your relationship with Intuition.

"Removing your head" techniques are a great way to lighten the load or reorganize your pack. You may revisit the "softcore" approaches when your brain is feeling especially wily. If it's your aim to travel more lightly, I recommend committing to steady, daily meditation or breathwork. Your pack will probably feel pounds lighter with as little as five minutes of "decapitation" per day. Mental dumping, or daily writing can also be highly effective. As always, do what you can and do what works for you.

Feel free to repeat the exercises that help you hone your navigational skills. Return to the sections that touch on your UNIQUE brand of communication whenever it serves or calls to you. The feeling realm, pain, or the mysterious pull of life might be your first language. However, learning to use your teachers, dreams, or omens as guideposts and trail markers might increase both your fluency and your confidence. Develop your strengths but continue to expand your repertoire.

Let what lights you up change and shift as you do. This may mean re-writing or reassessing which people, stories, books, places, or myths blow the fresh air of hope through your mind or carve out more room for love in your chest. Changes to this list might be rare, but bringing focus to your inspirations can help you absorb their radiance.

Lean into the magic. Allow yourself to love what you love. Leave the rest.

Over the course of the many "hit or miss" exercises, you had or will have a chance to practice speaking FOR you Intuition. Now it's time to practice speaking TO your Intuition. Name it if that feels less weird or more intimate. (For a period, I believe I called mine, "The Homie.") Write a letter to the entity formerly known as Intuition and share whatever feels... well, intuitive. You might compose a list of thank yous or reminisce about radical moments together. Circumstances considering, you might get a few frustrations or confessions off your chest. This letter could be an apology. If you're up for it (on this go around) make your Intuition some promises. If you've been ignoring her, what do you plan to do about it? How do you intend to nurture your relationship? Is there a call to adventure you aim to answer? Feel free to repeat this exercise whenever you so desire. The lines of communication are open. Go!

THE WORK

Dear Homie, Intuition, or _____,

I have a few things I'd like to say to you.

With Love, Gratitude, and Trust,

_____

SECTION 14: HAPPY TRAILS

"Goodbye, my Loooooooooooove!"

-Dumb and Dumber

My darling, my love, my beautiful, ridiculous, maddening human, you and your Intuition are off to the races. I hope you wear a frivolously large hat that makes you giggle at the absurdity of everything. I hope you use your Intuition to pick your horses or better yet, bet on yourself! I dream this workbook sparks a lifelong love affair similar to my relationship with the music of Ani Difranco, but deeper, richer, and even more magical and inspiring... if that's even possible. (Love Ani!) I hope you wipe the tears from the faces of your forsaken fragments and tenderly thank them for everything they've taught you. I hope you feel at home in your own mind. I wish you

329

the most fruitful of fuck-ups and ludicrous adventures, but (in the immortal words of the late, great Whitney Houston) above all this, I wish you love.

CONNECT AND CONTINUE

Book Buddy or Book Club

Intuition takes us deeper into ourselves. It also tends to bring us closer to one another. In addition to working through this book individually, you may want to revisit these exercises with a loved one or share what you've cataloged in a supportive, non-judgmental group setting. Insightful companions often see connections in floating dots of experiences. Spilling truth from your mouth to a room that sees, hears, and understands can be like dropping the final, magical ingredient into the bubbling cauldron of wellbeing and transformation.

Seek Out Other Teachers

This workbook could not exist without the immense research, skill, critical thinking, and creativity of other teachers, philosophers, coaches, psychologists, and fellow rebellious comrades. Some of my personal favorites whose work directly inspired this text include: Martha Beck, Joseph Campbell, Christopher "Hareesh" Wallis, and Rochelle Schieck. There are many more! If you'd like to follow a golden thread in the direction of a brilliant mind or playful teacher, I highly recommend the work of these individuals.

Work with an Intuitive Coach or Counselor

If you'd like to work with me directly to create a personal plan for intuitive development and receive individual coaching, I currently offer one on one sessions. Please visit yogigonerogue.com for more information. If you feel so inclined join the mailing list. Contact me to schedule a session at anikaspencer@hotmail.com. Happy Trails!

Made in the USA
Monee, IL
12 September 2022

13836032R00196